EMILY KLINTWORTH

YOUR
COSMIC
COMPASS

Do-It-Yourself
Yearly Astrological Planner

Other Schiffer Books by the Author:

Claiming Your Power Through Astrology: A Spiritual Workbook
ISBN: 978-0-7643-5272-0

Other Schiffer Books on Related Subjects:

The Beginner's Guide to Astrology: Class Is in Session. Dusty Bunker
ISBN: 978-0-7643-5330-7

Astrology & Relationships. Mary Devlin
ISBN: 978-0-9149-1877-6

Copyright © 2018 by Emily Klintworth

Library of Congress Control Number: 2018934596

All rights reserved. No part of this work may be reproduced or used in any form or by any means—graphic, electronic, or mechanical, including photocopying or information storage and retrieval systems—without written permission from the publisher.

The scanning, uploading, and distribution of this book or any part thereof via the Internet or any other means without the permission of the publisher is illegal and punishable by law. Please purchase only authorized editions and do not participate in or encourage the electronic piracy of copyrighted materials.

"Red Feather Mind Body Spirit" logo is a registered trademark of Schiffer Publishing, Ltd.

Designed by Molly Shields
Cover design by Matthew Goodman

Type set in MasonSerif/Adobe Garamond

ISBN: 978-0-7643-5593-6
Printed in United States of America

Published by Red Feather Mind, Body, Spirit
An imprint of Schiffer Publishing, Ltd.
4880 Lower Valley Road
Atglen, PA 19310
Phone: (610) 593-1777; Fax: (610) 593-2002
E-mail: Info@schifferbooks.com
Web: www.redfeathermbs.com

For our complete selection of fine books on this and related subjects, please visit our website at www.schifferbooks.com. You may also write for a free catalog.

Schiffer Publishing's titles are available at special discounts for bulk purchases for sales promotions or premiums. Special editions, including personalized covers, corporate imprints, and excerpts, can be created in large quantities for special needs. For more information, contact the publisher.

We are always looking for people to write books on new and related subjects. If you have an idea for a book, please contact us at:
proposals@schifferbooks.com.

I dedicate this book to my two beautiful, perfect children, Jack and Lily. This yearly spiritual guidebook was written for those on the path of awakening, and both of you were my muses. I wrote to you, and in so doing I wrote to the world. You are my lovely fiery spirits who are so full of life and passion: Jack, my Aries Warrior, and Lily, my Sagittarius Philosopher. What seems the inevitable path never actually feels inevitable as it unfolds. Each step of your life, you will need to push through fear until one day you arrive. Please know that I am always with you, loving you, cheering you on, and holding a space for you to live the life you dream of in your heart (that is absolutely the life you were meant to live). I love you forever, through all space and time.

Contents

Introduction

We are living in a powerful time. A time when the veil to the other side is being lifted, providing us with more opportunity for spiritual growth than ever before. This opportunity is unique and is opening the door to further development of our self, as well as our group consciousness as a species. We have embraced this journey, have learned many spiritual lessons along the way, and are ready now, more than ever, to push even further into connecting with our natural birthright to live our lives to their full potential.

I would like to emphasize that no big movement forward has ever occurred without the little movement forward each day. Regardless of where you are at on your path, this book promises to deliver on insight and instruction. This book is a spiritual guidebook, one that is uniquely tailored to you that will allow you to explore the cosmic conditions that surround one specific year of your life (from birthdate to birthdate). Through this exploration, you will be provided with valuable insights, meditations, mantras, and advice. Each chapter is rich with ancient knowledge that can be applied to your life. With each bit of wisdom that you receive, you will be able to complete the Vision Sheet for your year. This Vision Sheet is designed to assist you in creating your very own cosmic calendar, anchoring in all the knowledge you gain throughout these lessons. The book can be used repeatedly, exploring any year of your choosing. Each time you come back, you will discover that the cosmic conditions have shifted and your spiritual guidance has evolved.

My mission in this life is to assist the individual in taking back their power and teaching them how to consciously steer their own life. There is no better translator for this information in your life than YOU. In order to complete this spiritual adventure, you must download your Cosmic Navigator from www.absolutelyastrology.com. To do this, you must enter your date of birth, time of birth, and location of birth (I cannot stress enough that the time of birth must be accurate). Once that information is entered, you will need to select the location of where you will be located for the majority of the year explored (this may be different from your place of birth for obvious reasons), along with that specific year. The foundation of this journey depends on the astrological Solar Return Chart. Thus, the accuracy is completely dependent on the birth data that is provided.

All of this information is necessary in creating the energetic blueprint for your upcoming year. In this book, there is nothing you need to memorize—all you need is your Cosmic Navigator. Throughout each chapter, you will be asked to reference your Cosmic Navigator to determine the cosmic conditions unique to you—this is how your adventure unfolds. Yes, the Cosmic Navigator can pull up the cosmic blueprint of any year you choose going forward and backward in time. Reminding us that the past, present, and future are ever blending and making their impressions known. Follow your heart and explore whatever needs exploring; there is no better captain for this journey than YOU.

Visit WWW.ABSOLUTELYASTROLOGY.COM now to DOWNLOAD YOUR Cosmic Navigator, Vision Sheet and Sample Vision Sheet!

CHAPTER ONE

Discovering Your Cosmic Compass

Every individual has a destiny, a path they hoped they'd embrace and realize during their earthly incarnation. There were certainly specific lessons you wanted to learn, karma you wanted to balance, and goals you wanted to achieve. Each year of your life has a specific outline, and there will inevitably be a main topic, points of concern to address, and an overall theme that develops as the year unfolds. This cosmic blueprint is the key to unlocking the full potential of your year. Great things happen through small yet great actions—we are capable of these actions every day of our lives. If you are seeking guidance, direction, and encouragement, then this book is for you. It can be your very own cosmic compass that will assist you in achieving your goals, staying up to speed with your manifestations, and preparing you for the spiritual lessons locked within each year of your life.

As crazy as it sounds, there is a cosmic blueprint that will allow you to align with the energetic unseen forces of this world. For those who are eager, ready, and willing, this book will be your compass while you explore the potential of your life through each year. The year is reflective of YOU specifically and runs from birthday to birthday. Your path evolves and reveals itself in harmony with the Sun. When the Sun returns to the same position in the zodiac it occupied at the moment of your birth, your path elevates and new challenges, gifts, and opportunities become available to you.

It is important to understand that astrologers do not believe that the planets are making things happen to you. We believe that the celestial circumstances are a reflection of what is happening rather than the cause. Perhaps this metaphor will help paint the picture in a way that you may truly understand the gift that is astrology. If it is raining and water is falling down to the Earth from the sky, we can easily see that what is happening in the sky is reflected on the Earth. The clouds above are changed in color, shape, and size, and the weather and temperature may also have altered. As the rain comes down to the Earth, it will inevitably impact the circumstances below. It will add moisture and water to the soil, grass, and land. This movement above provides opportunity below. Now, let's say that a seed was just planted in the soil. The rain is obviously very good for this seed, and its impact would be received, the result being that the potential of the seed will be nourished. We cannot say that the cloud above is making the seed grow, because that is not the complete story. We also cannot say that the cloud put the seed in the earth because that also is not the whole story. But what we can say is that what's happening below (the water nourishing the seed) is providing the seed with the opportunity to grow through the circumstances that were reflected above.

The moment the Sun returns to the specific location in the zodiac where it was located when you were born (down to the degree, minute, and second) represents your true birthday, and this is called your Solar (Sun) Return. This typically occurs within one day of your actual birthdate each year. As the Sun returns to this exact position yearly, your life elevates and the potential for the next year is revealed. This is your cosmic blueprint; the astrological conditions at this exact moment in time reflect from the heavens that which is about to occur on Earth. The Solar Return Chart is always drawn to this exact moment in time, and it reflects the 12 months to come.

The information you are about to receive is sacred, developed over thousands of years, and is extremely occult. It has been passed down throughout the ages and is now being passed down to you. This is because in one way or another, you are ready. There is truly no other way you could have arrived at a moment when you are reading these words if you weren't. The information you will be provided with IS the pivotal information you need into your upcoming year, and it will provide you with direction, helping you express the full potential of YOUR year.

The Solar Return Chart

It's important to have the Cosmic Navigator ready to go before you dive in and begin this journey. You will need to select the city that you will be located in for the majority of the year you are exploring. This means if you are exploring the year 2015, and you will be living the majority of this year in San Francisco, run the chart for San Francisco (regardless if you happen to be in Los Angeles to celebrate your birthday during that time). The Solar Return Chart is not concerned with the city of birth, but with the city where the energy will be taken in throughout the year. This means you will always select the city that you will spend the majority of your time in for that year.

The Vision Sheet

It is very important that you anchor in all of this new knowledge as you proceed through the chapters. Life is about working smarter, not harder. If you have arrived in a moment when this knowledge is being delivered to you, it's up to you to anchor it in to your life and year. You will be able to download your Vision Sheet and Cosmic Navigator from AbsolutelyAstrology.com. The Vision Sheet will specifically capture the information you need as you complete your cosmic calendar.

The Cosmic Navigator

You'll notice that the locations of all the planets in the Cosmic Navigator are written out (word for word) and are extremely easy to understand and interpret. If your Moon was in Cancer, it will be written as such (no need to decipher astrological glyphs). I recommend that you print out your Cosmic Navigator and keep it secured in this book. In each chapter, you will explore the conditions based on YOUR specific cosmic blueprint for the year, as outlined in your Cosmic Navigator (just like a good, old-fashioned choose-your-own adventure).

We are already in the habit of celebrating each year of our lives on the date of our birth, and I would like to make a personal suggestion on how you can honor this sacred passage of time. Each year, start to celebrate your birthday in a three-day fashion. This will allow you to pay tribute to the three dimensions of time that we experience: past, present, and future. The day before you celebrate your birthday, pay tribute to the moments in the PAST that have brought you to your current circumstance. This can be done in many ways: an altar with photographs from various time periods in your life, writing in your journal, or even a simple five-minute meditation before you fall asleep at night. Here you will pay honor to the forces that brought you into this world by exploring your accomplishments, setbacks, gifts, and limitations.

On the day that you are accustomed to celebrating your birthday, choose to surround yourself with the people and life-force energy that is expansive in your life. This is a day to celebrate the love that is in you and around you. This can be done through a party, a family celebration, or in any fashion that brings you into the PRESENT moment. Here you are taking in the perfect circumstance that is in harmony with your current spiritual state.

The next day after you have celebrated your birthday, I would like you to focus on the FUTURE and the year that is to come. On this day, I hope that you will seek to know the cosmic conditions of your life during the upcoming year. I would like you to use that day to read and discover the potential of your year through this book. As you complete this journey, you will use the Vision Sheet to record the valuable insights and to set specific goals for your year. There are no words to describe the gifts waiting for you through astrology, and I am honored to be able to guide you as you access your cosmic compass and reveal the energy that is waiting for you!

Vision Sheet Instructions
Basic Vision Sheet Setup

Step 1:

The Vision Sheet will support you in setting up your yearly astrological planner. As you discovered in this chapter, the year is unique to the individual and correlates with their birthdate. To ensure that you are looking at the right time frame, please take a moment to determine the year you would like to explore.

Part 1:

The yearly chart runs from birthdate to birthdate. A chart that is created for 2017 will in fact correlate to the birthdate in 2017 to the birthdate in 2018. Take a moment to decide what year you would like to explore (I recommend looking at the upcoming year if your birthday is within 2–3 months of when you are completing the Vision Sheet).

Part 2:

Once you determine the year you will be exploring, you will write the time frame into the blank innermost circle on the front page of your Vision Sheet. This will ensure that you always know what month and year you are looking at. For instance, if you are exploring the year 2017, you will write in the time frame, 2017–2018. Please see the example Vision Sheet on Pg. XXX for reference as you move through this journey.

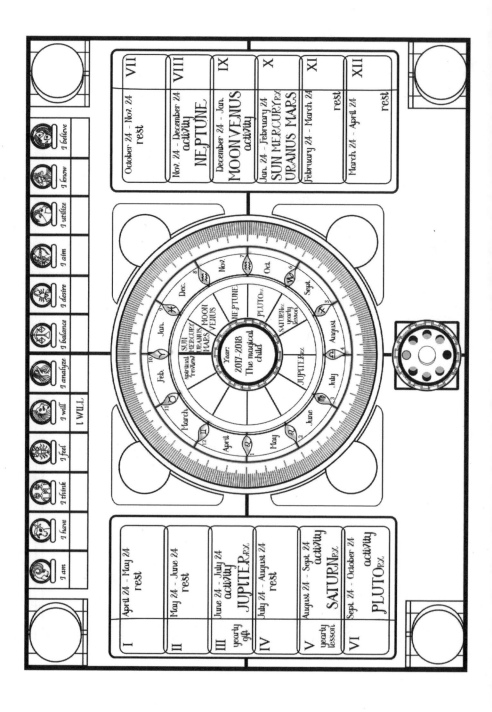

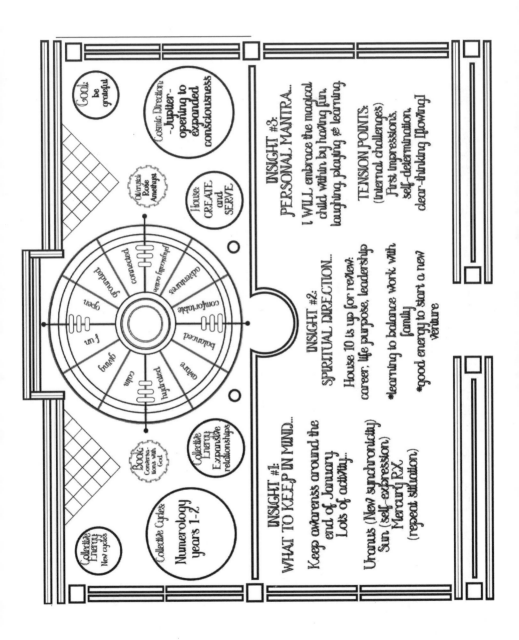

Goal:
be grateful

Cosmic Direction:
–Jupiter–
opening to
expanded
consciousness

Crystals:
Rose
Amethyst

House:
CREATE
and
SERVE

Book:
Conversa-
tions with
God

Collective Energy:
Expansive
relationships

Collective Cycles:
Numerology
years 1–2

Collective Energy:
New cycles

connected · playful · physical · adventures · comfortable · balanced · nature · calm · hydrated · giving · fun · open · grounded

INSIGHT #3:
PERSONAL MANTRA...

I WILL embrace the magical
child within by having fun,
laughing, playing & learning

TENSION POINTS:
(internal challenges)
First impressions,
self-determination,
clear-thinking [flowing]

INSIGHT #2:
SPIRITUAL DIRECTION...

House 10 is up for review:
career, life purpose, leadership

*learning to balance work with
family

*good energy to start a new
venture

INSIGHT #1:
WHAT TO KEEP IN MIND...

Keep awareness around the
end of January.
Lots of activity...

Uranus (New synchronicity)
Sun (self-expression)
Mercury RX
(repeat situation)

15

CHAPTER TWO

Creating Your Cosmic Calendar

Have you ever just felt lazy? Like nothing was happening and you had no motivation to make things happen? Or have you ever felt like you were on fire, productive and ready to conquer the world? I'm sure there have been time frames in your life when you truly felt the presence of being and were filled with love. These times are always contrasted with the more constrictive moments, ones that make you question your existence, purpose, and the point of being at all.

Just as your physical body breathes, so does your year. We of course are not taught this, but we feel it. There are constrictive moments where you feel like you don't want to do anything at all, where you begin to question and demand answers (and those answers simply won't come). Then there is the time of complete flow where you feel at harmony with your path, the world, and everyone around you. These are natural patterns that we all experience, but the resistance arises when we pull back and try to battle with the natural ebb and flow of *being* and creation.

Perhaps you may hit some major upset in your business seemingly out of nowhere, and this is AFTER being extraordinarily successful. Or maybe you went from dating frequently to what you can only refer to as a dry spell. Or potentially, your very positive relationship has started to require a lot more work. All of this can feel very constrictive within you, and without proper guidance and understanding you may begin to unnecessarily question yourself and your life.

On the flip side of this constrictive energy, you may have just landed your dream job that you never in a million years thought you would get, or you finally met your dream mate on a blind date you'd avoided for a year, or you randomly discovered a new hobby that fills you with passion (and you are naturally pretty good at it). This would mark the expansive moments of your year when you experience flow, active creation, and action forward in the physical world.

ALL of this is natural, normal, and a part of the growth cycle of your Soul. The only thing that is not normal is that we are taught to fight it, resist it, and question it. Rather than using the constrictive times to relax, regroup, and get clear, you most likely begin to panic and unintentionally cause inner energetic resistance. You panic because you haven't been taught about the inner ebb and flow of life. You've been trained to constantly need to be working toward something, achieving some goal, and you feel guilty when you aren't experiencing that pull forward. All of a sudden, as if on some weird universal theatrical queue, the inner questioning begins

- Am I burned out?
- Am I in the wrong relationship?
- Did I choose the wrong career?
- Am I a failure?
- What am I doing wrong?
- Why isn't anything happening?

The questions begin and they aren't always guiding you in the right direction. How could they? Those questions exist based on what you've been taught, and you've been taught that non-action is not an action. This of course is false because everything is in motion (even the inanimate chair is still moving through space on the Earth).

You've been taught that to rest too much is lazy and that you should rest only enough so that you can keep up with the world. The craziest thing of all is that there is never a point of arrival where you have officially achieved all that you were meant to achieve in your life. That elusive point of accomplishment pulls us forward, but it is a mirage that keeps moving just out of our reach (you never could or never will arrive at a final destination of absolute growth).

Life isn't about burning yourself out in the pursuit of reaching this elusive destination. It's about coming face to face with the truth of *being* and learning to love and enjoy these simple processes of growth and *Life*.

Here is how you will typically experience the constrictive and expansive energy throughout your year:

Constrictive:

The constrictive energies create an inward pull into yourself and a reversal from a focus on the external world into the inner world. There is a pull for rest, relaxation, renewal, and refocusing. This is often met with a feeling of slowing down, moving backward, or a lack of a specific direction you need to go in. This is ultimately about assessing your life experiences to date, taking time to rest the physical body as much as you can, and allowing the world to play catch up with all the energetic changes that took place during your last expansive energy phase.

When the energy in your yearly chart supports rest, renewal, and getting clear, choose activities that allow you to feel at home in your own body and Soul. This could be meditation, massage, vacation, yoga, etc. It's taking a form of non-action that allows you to fully relax into who you are and where you are at. Non-action is still movement forward, but it lacks all levels of attachment (because the non-action is complete on its own). Here you are to become focused on the very act of *being*.

Expansive:

The expansive energies create an outward pull into the Physical World and a focus on wanting to do, be, and live. There is a pull to interact with other people, experience new circumstances, achieve goals, and ultimately be expanding your life experience. You will feel more social and you will find conversations easier to participate in. Circumstances, events, and people important to your path often arrive during these active time frames.

Use this time to sign up for new activities, participate in events, and get together with the people you love. This is about stepping into the unknown and stretching outside your comfort zone. This time period requires you to take action in the physical world and a step forward in whatever direction inspires you (and yes, it is okay to take action forward with deeper aligned intentions during this time).

Both the constrictive and expansive energies will be experienced internally through emotions, feelings, and state of mind, and externally through new circumstances entering your life.

Before you learn more about your year, I've found that it is very helpful to set up your calendar to provide you with a point of reference for all the information that is to come. This is why I will be having you dive straight into setting up your calendar on your Vision Sheet now.

Vision Sheet Instructions
Setting up your Cosmic Calendar

Step 1:

You will first start by defining the time periods for your yearly calendar.

Part 1:

On the front page of your Vision Sheet, there is a circle chart in the center with rectangles on either side. There are 6 rectangles on either side of this circle and together, they correlate with the 12 months of your year (6 x 2 = 12). Starting with the rectangle on the left labeled "I," write your birthdate into the blank rectangle connected to the label "I." For example, if you were born on February 21, you would write in "February 21" into the empty rectangle. There is an example Vision Sheet on pages 14–15 for further guidance as needed.

Part 2:

Each rectangle represents a time span of roughly 30 days. To complete the time frame for the first rectangle, you will need to add roughly 30 days to the date you just entered in step 1.

For example, if you were born on February 21, your first time span in the 1st rectangle would be "February 21st–March 21st." Write in the time span to the "I" rectangle now.

Step 2:

You will complete the time frames for the rest of your yearly calendar.

Part 1:

Take the last date you entered in rectangle "I" and enter it as the starting date in the second rectangle, numbered "II."

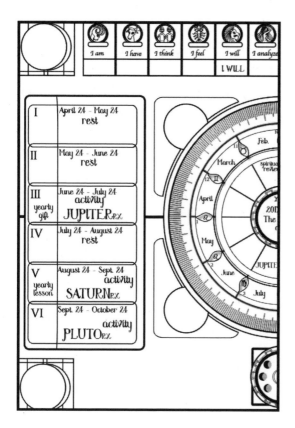

Part 2:

You will follow the same process as before and add roughly 30 days to this date. From our example above, your time frame for rectangle II would read "March 21–April 21."

Part 3:

Continue this pattern until you have created your 12-month breakdown for your cosmic calendar.

STEP 3:

In table 1, column 1, of your Cosmic Navigator, you will find the names of the relevant planets and sensitive points you will be writing into your calendar. How the planets fall into the different time periods of your year reflects the energetic patterning you will be experiencing throughout your upcoming year. There is a different pattern for every year of your life.

We will start first by determining the location of the Sun and then entering it into the appropriate rectangle in your calendar.

Part 1:

In table 1, locate the Sun in column 1, and then look to column 4, labeled "Annual House." The number under column 4 corresponds to the astrological house location, and you will be using these numbers to match them to the roman numerals in your calendar. Once you locate the number in the "Annual House" column, match it to the appropriate rectangle (using the roman numerals) and then write the planet name into the larger connected rectangle.

This will show you what time periods are being influenced by which planets. Note: The planets are distributed into the various houses, and you may have some houses without any planets at all (we will explore the meaning of this shortly).

For example, if the Sun is in the Annual House 4, you will write "Sun" into the larger rectangle that is labeled IV. This would indicate that the influence of the Sun is strongest during the time frame that it is connected to in your calendar.

Part 2:

Using your Cosmic Navigator and columns 1 and 4, you will place the remaining planets into your cosmic calendar: Moon, Mercury, Venus, Mars, Jupiter, Saturn, Uranus, Neptune, and Pluto. You can notate if the planet is retrograde by including "Rx" when you write it into the rectangle. The retrograde influence will create an inner pull and what may feel like backward motion in your life or that you are facing a similar experience to one you have faced before. Be sure to double check that you have not missed any of the planets as you complete this process (there will be a total of 10).

Note: You do not enter the Ascendant or Midheaven listed under Sensitive Points.

STEP 4:

By now you have a very nice visual of how the energy is spread out for your year through the energetic patterning. We will take one more step and begin to record the bigger patterns to support you in navigating these energies throughout your year.

Part 1:

Rectangles with no planets represent time frames when the energy tends to be more constrictive, and is typically a time when you will want to consciously choose to take it easy, slow down, and relax. Locate the rectangles that have no planets and write in the word "relax" to remind yourself to honor the slower moments of the year by regrouping, relaxing, and taking care of yourself.

Part 2:

Rectangles with planets represent time frames of activity in your life. Locate the rectangles that have planets or sensitive points and write in the word "activity" to remind yourself that you can align with the energy of the planet by remaining aware and ready to experience the energy as it shows up.

What if the deep Soul satisfaction we crave doesn't come from achieving anything, but merely surfaces from learning to live with the natural cycles of *being*? We have long heard the metaphor of the seasons of life. What if the true secret of life is to make the most of your seasons? To live in harmony with the energy around you regardless of experiencing an inner winter and a feeling like you need to isolate, or an inner summer when you feel like you need to shine?

When you create your Cosmic Calendar, you will begin to bring into your perception exactly what you need to be empowered and to rise to the potential of your year. These energetic pulls of constriction and expansion you experience are always equal in power and potential. Neither of these energetic pulls should make you feel off, out of flow, or as if you are not in tune with the dynamics of your life.

Although we are more likely to feel internal resistance when the constrictive energies pull us to rest and restore (due to our upbringing and culture), we can still feel resistance during expansive states of growth as well. The rule of thumb is that whenever you are working in the opposite direction of the growth currents in your life, you will experience some form of inner resistance. This is because we all exist within a much-larger consciousness (call it The One, The Universe, God, Source), and when we flow with its life force we feel magnificent and in harmony. When you move against it, you will often feel frustrated, annoyed, stagnant, and off.

I somewhat jokingly and with a bit of raw honesty call these moments of life getting hit by the spiritual two-by-four (an energetic feeling of being slapped over and over again by the Universe because you're going in the wrong direction of your life current). If you are ever experiencing this inner condition of internal resistance, I recommend that you look at your cosmic calendar. If you feel off and see that you are in a constrictive time frame of rest, I would recommend resting, regrouping, and getting clear. However, you may find that you are in an expansive time frame, and this will ultimately be very confusing for you (how can you be in expansion and feel resistance to that wild ride?). If and when this happens, this is when you will need to call upon some deeper Soul work (check out my energetic pivoting technique in this chapter).

The moments of greatest constrictive energy give way to the moments of rest, renewal, and observation. The moments of greatest expansive energy give way to the moments of growth, passion, and inspiration. The trick to all of this is that there is no better or worse, or right or wrong, with this constriction or expansion inherent to your year (I'm sure many would argue this, but truth is truth). The expansive stage is just as important as the constrictive phase, because what can you breathe out, if you don't breathe in?

Spiritual Guidance
The Energetic Pivoting Technique

Energetic pivoting is a technique that allows you to shift the inner current of your Inner Speaker (the thinking—you chatting away in your head). Use this technique whenever you feel off or out of alignment to pivot yourself back into the current of your life force.

The thought processes that occur in your head through the thinking mind are often experienced as a series of questions and answers. Your thinking mind creates a question and then it answers it, over and over again. It can do this with words as the Inner Narrator in your head (the speaking voice within you), or it can play this out visually with a complementary movie scene to drive home its messages.

The beauty is that because of this question/answer dynamic, you can pivot your own internal energy by merely switching the questions you are asking yourself. When you ask yourself new questions, you will inevitably get new answers. Since your thoughts create an energetic vibration that impacts your whole auric field, you can literally take this tiny pivot internally and impact your external environment.

Let's look at an example.

I have a friend, Mary, who expresses her disappointment and struggle with relationships but is very much interested in finding a compatible mate. She feels stuck internally and just can't seem to feel good anymore about how she is approaching this part of her life (and she can't stop thinking about it either). She feels frustrated and annoyed and uses the word "stagnant" to describe how she feels. She finds herself in a space of frustrating agony that she is dating the same type of person over and over again, and it isn't working out.

Mary decides to look at her cosmic calendar and finds that she is actually in a state of expansion and a time frame when the Sun, Mercury, and Venus are present. She reasons with her logical mind that she feels off because she is going against this current of expansion. She recognizes the questions she had been replaying over and over again in her mind: What am I doing wrong? Why doesn't anyone love me? What do I need to do to change myself to make me more lovable?

She mentioned how annoyed and powerless she felt because these questions were so negative and she didn't even realize she was doing this. Mary struggled to get to the new questions, but she persevered. She first started by writing down the old questions that she had hardly realized she had been playing over and over again in her mind. To get to the new questions, she literally made them up and made sure that they felt positive and expansive. She knew that it wouldn't just switch automatically, so she wrote them down on the piece of paper. The moment she wrote them down, she felt her energy start to move in a new direction and felt a wave of inspiration sweep through her.

She replaced the original questions that her MIND had created with new ones of her own CONSCIOUS choosing: How can I always be my authentic self and feel safe in relationships? How can I choose to trust others and seek to find their goodness? How can I start to slowly open my heart in my friendships so that I can continue to fully open?

She particularly liked the question she came up with regarding her friendships. Based on this new question (and knowing she was in an expansive period of activity), she decided to move in that direction. Because of this, she moved to connect with and plan a dinner with her closest group of girlfriends. This is the moment when Mary experienced the first part of energetic pivoting. The official movement began the moment she stepped in this new direction with the current of the life force, and things felt different!

Perhaps at that dinner she opened up to her friends and shared from her heart (huge relief with this small but important action). At this dinner she might have received some really great advice, have learned about a new online dating website, have been set up on a blind date, have been invited to a work party by a friend, etc. The truth is that there are always a multitude of ways that energy can express (this is the Law of Potentiality).

What's important is that Mary FEELS different internally and has shifted out of her internal energetic resistance. It all started when she consciously decided to change the questions she was asking herself and took inspired action. She had no attachment to the outcome because she was focused on the feeling within her, and that had now become her guiding light. Remember, energy always has an endless amount of ways that it can express and it will ALWAYS meet you exactly where you are at. It is never about taking risky, careless actions. It is about finding the space of inspiration and ease where you can confidently explore and move forward in your life.

CHAPTER THREE

Important Turning Points

Just like the plot thickens in a great movie, so do the energies of your year. There will be a moment of deepest expansion and also a moment of deepest constriction. These twin forces work to support you in your Soul growth and development in your life. The only part of your being that fights this dynamic is your personality / Ego / thinking mind. To empower you to challenge the "go! go! go!" attitude of the mind, it's important to see the energies and allow yourself to let go and relax when it is appropriate.

It's kind of crazy, but I can be doing a reading for someone, and the moment I tell them that they are in a constrictive time of release, I can hear them take a long, deep exhale and express a sigh of relief. I can literally feel them let go, and then their energy changes instantaneously. In many ways, the Ego needs convincing in the form of permission to let go and relax.

Although you absolutely can provide that permission in the now moment through your own knowing and just let go, we all know it's just not that easy. Your mind will keep trying to calculate ways forward and things you need to do. When the energy isn't supporting those initiatives, it's easy to turn in on yourself and feel not good enough or that you are doing something wrong. The true issue lies in the deeper subconscious mind that will continually try to fix and control. There is certainly a reason employers limit the amount of hours their employees work (and it isn't just because they care about your well-being). An overworked person doesn't perform as well. An overworked Ego is exactly the same. If you're someone who has a constantly thinking mind that never takes a break, you have yourself a problem that fits this exact scenario. The solution isn't in finding a solution, but in taking time to relax, let go, and stop problem hunting.

The Ego is not bad and does not need to be destroyed. Spiritual techniques that focus on the destruction of the Ego have fallen for the Ego's greatest last play! It is another Ego (created by the Ego) that now needs your undivided attention to overcome, fight, battle, and destroy. When you realize that the Ego is simply a construct of thought, you are able to see the score. Thought + Thought = More Thought.

The good news is that when you actually physically see your energy calendar, it's a good slap in the face to the Ego. Believe it or not, the Ego is actually happy to let go! Think of it as the overworked employee who hasn't been home in about a year's worth of time. It keeps making mistakes but doesn't realize all that time has passed, and it is stuck. The more it tries, the more it ultimately fails because it lost perspective. Please, please, please keep in mind that the Ego is neither bad nor good. The issue is that it is constantly wanting to work, and it wasn't designed to run the show (your heart/mind united does this from a completely different space).

The calendar you've created has already shown you where the energy will be expansive and where it will be constrictive. All the planets relate to different forces you experience internally. The focus of your being is to accept, unite, understand, and support that which happens within you. There is much more to you than the thoughts you think in your head. On your journey you will continue to meet different aspects of your personality and learn more and more. This continually happens because you are a multidimensional *being*. There is no "arriving" as the linear mind would have you believe.

Seeing where the planets sit throughout your year is a great way to understand and work with their dynamics. It has been my personal experience that the energetic calendar you are creating right now is absolutely spot on. This knowledge is due to the responses I received when providing astrology readings to clients. Yes, you have to stretch your mind and take a few minutes to read/understand it all. BUT the energy and focus you put into this process will support you in ways you can't even possibly understand until later on down the road.

By simply gaining awareness around these forces, you can more easily align to and work with them. This is why you are going to continue to look at and understand the energetic patterning of your year.

Vision Sheet Instructions
Deeper Exploration of the Energetic Patterning of Your Year

Step 1:

Now it's time to mark and determine the culminating constrictive energy that corresponds to when the most significant *lesson* of your year will take place.

Part 1:

Locate Saturn in the rectangles and write in the words "Yearly Lesson" under the roman numeral. There is always a nugget of wisdom to be absorbed during this time frame if you are able to expand your perspective and grasp it.

Step 2:

Now it's time to mark and determine the culminating expansive energy of the year where the *gift* of the year will most likely show up.

Part 1:

Locate Jupiter in the rectangles and write in the words "Yearly Gift" under the roman numeral. There is always a great form of expansion that takes place through the energy of Jupiter (whether you recognize it or not).

Step 3:

There is a Planet Key in this chapter on page 33 that gives you an idea of the energetics and insight of each planet. As you complete this last step, take some time to refer to the Planet Key. Your focus now is on being able to see, feel, and understand the energy of your year.

Part 1:

Take a few minutes (or more) to get acquainted with your year. Visually take in the energetic patterning and begin to discover the impact of each planet, using the Planet Key on page 33. Begin to trust your natural intuition about the energetic patterning you see inherent to your year. How does it make you feel? What excites you about your year? What intrigues you?

Part 2:

Take a moment to jot down any insights that come to you in the section, labeled "Insights" on the back of your Vision Sheet. I recommend looking for a specific month that speaks to you, reading about the meaning and piecing it together for yourself. Then you will write an insight and label it "Insight 1." Feel free to use the example Vision Sheet for reference.

IMPORTANT! I know how easy it is to skip over the parts where you journal and write down insights. You are excited and want to get to the big stuff; it might even feel boring to do this. But you don't know what you don't know. You may not see the importance **now** of writing these insights down, but I need you to trust me on this—I've been doing this a long time. While my clients love the readings and are always inspired, it's the moment they come back to what I wrote or said later that takes their breathe away. What is coming to you **now** will serve you **later**. I have no other way to express this: please write the insights and take your time.

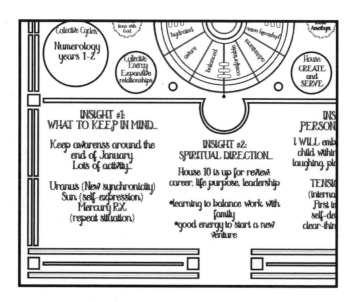

Planet Key for Cosmic Calendar

SUΠ [Expaɴsive]:

The Sun rules the individual personality expression and marks a time frame when you are stepping deeper into alignment with your true self. There may be an event that occurs that pushes you to step deeper into your own voice and authentic self.

ΠOOΠ [Expaɴsive]:

The Moon rules the instinctual and emotional patterns inherent to your being through multiple lifetimes. This is often an emotionally heightened period, and you will experience the deeper connections (or lack of connections) that are currently being expressed in your life.

MERCURY [Expaɴsive]:

Mercury rules communication and thinking and thus elevates the processes of your thinking mind. This is a time frame of learning new skills or feeling very curious to step outside your normal comfort zone. Take the leap to move forward through learning or taking an initiative to start interesting conversations.

VEΠUS [Expaɴsive]:

Venus rules your heart and influences your relationships and the things you hold dear. This time frame often revolves around wanting to express your love and uphold your values. There is often a nurturing instinct that begins to surface, and this can be felt toward family, friends, acquaintances, and even strangers. This is a great time for charitable work or donations.

MARS [Coɴstrictive or Expaɴsive]:

Mars acts as a trigger for events to occur that will often allow you new opportunities (or push you out of stagnant ones). There can be a burning fire within to change a set of circumstances during this time. Make sure that you honor the fire for the passion and not the impulsivity.

JUPITER [Expansive]:

Jupiter rules your spiritual development and supports whatever growth is necessary to get you to the next stage of awakening. This is the gift of the year, and you will experience this both internally and externally. Keep your awareness high and stay open to whatever shows up in your life. Practice gratitude and compassion as this time frame unfolds.

SATURN [Constrictive]:

Saturn creates the necessary pressure and tension that will push you through any obstacle that may be holding you back. This is the time frame of the yearly lesson, and you most likely will feel it (sometimes it's a harder energy to understand because it often works on your energetic blind spot). This can seem daunting at first and may leave you in a state of inner resistance. Use the Energetic Pivoting Technique on page 25 in this chapter if you struggle to align with and understand the lesson from Saturn.

URANUS [Neutral]:

Uranus causes quick and immediate change in circumstances and acts as a jolt of energy. This energy is hard to prepare for but must not be taken for granted when it shows up. This could be the moment you bump into someone and accidentally spill coffee on them, only to find out that you have a common goal that supports one another. Uranus is curious like this, so stay open and lose any judgment you have around random or weird events (if you don't, you'll lose the synchronicity).

NEPTUNE [Neutral]:

Neptune is often the blind spot where we want to imagine that things are different than they are. This is a time frame when you will need to sharpen these skills and seek to see the truth as it is. Eternal truth knows that there is goodness and light in all *beings*, but the truth of the moment is that they may not be expressing it. Honor each person you come into contact with for their inherent worth, but don't get sucked down into somebody else's mess.

PLUTO [Constrictive]:

Pluto causes deeper personal transformation and often allows you to step deeper into your own power (whether you want to or not). If Pluto is close to other constrictive planets such as Saturn (meaning they are in the same time frame), you will experience a blending of the two energies, and it may magnify your transformation. If Pluto is next to an expansive planet (like the Sun), it can help take the edge off a bit and support a smoother transformation. No matter the energetic patterning, Pluto supports your use of personal power (and developing it in a way that serves the whole).

IV

CHAPTER FOUR

GROWTH THROUGH THE SUN

(THE SELF)

As you complete your cosmic calendar, you will begin to see the energetic patterning the planets are taking on throughout your year. Each year when the Sun returns to the place it was in at the time of your birth, you begin a brand-new cycle of life. If you can imagine for a moment a never-ending slinky, you will begin to understand the cyclical nature of growth throughout not only your physical life here on Earth, but beyond into the spiritual realm where you exist as an energetic being.

In the case of the never-ending slinky, it would be possible to view it from an angle that makes it appear to look like a circle, but this would be missing the eternal truth. The truth is that it is actually an infinite spiral out into infinity. As you complete a cycle of growth each year, you have moved on to the next cycle of the slinky circle.

If you imagine a squished-up slinky with virtually no space between each set of the rings, you are seeing a year in which the individual is fighting the forces of the unseen and is essentially going uphill. This is also when people experience what feels like an energetic loop and what is referred to as the wheel of karma. The tighter the slinky, the denser the vibrations that are held within. It is the vibrations that are held within that create the dimensions of *being* (dimensions are really just differing perspectives).

The third dimension is a space of dense frequencies within where you feel like everything "out there" is happening to you. From this space, you don't know or realize that you are interacting/influencing the energy you experience "out there." All you know is that you feel separate, isolated, and like you didn't get invited to the party where everyone else is.

Within you, there will be a little spark and belief that there must be more than meets the eye. This is why you will start to seek knowledge and to understand what is really going on. This is bringing you to what is often referred to as the fourth dimension. This perspective is felt like a bridge, and you will exist in a space that has you toggling back and forth between the third and fifth dimensions. This is where all the inner drama and battling and much of the suffering takes place. One minute you are in complete harmony, and the next . . . you fall. From this space in the fourth dimension, you are working to create the pathway between the mind and heart. You work here to release the fear and lower aspects of *being*: judgment, betrayal, jealousy, greed, fear, etc.

The majority of the collective is currently in the transition/bridge phase of the fourth dimension. The slinky rings are important to work with because the more you fight to control, the tighter and slower you move through this. I'm not sure where you are, but most people I meet (including myself the majority of the time) are working things out in the fourth dimension. Much suffering does occur throughout this process, and it is mostly felt within.

IF you were to get really, really honest with yourself, what would you say about your inner world? Are you accepting of yourself? Do you look at, examine, and work to understand and integrate your thoughts? Or do you try to change them as quickly as you can and distract yourself with mindless tasks (in an effort to escape the battle within your own mind)?

This is a part of the evolving Soul path, and everyone must walk through it. It's a damn shame that there isn't more humor, camaraderie, and connection to support us as we do. Please don't ever be ashamed of having that inner experience! You are definitely not alone, and if you have one hell of a time trying to maintain control/perspective of the crazy that is in the mind, congrats! You have begun the process to integrate and release all that no longer serves you. The biggest hiccup is when you continue to run, hide, and try to escape the process.

There are endless cycles of being, and to see and understand them through the metaphor of the never-ending slinky can hopefully help you in understanding all of this. For me, there was so much written, but not much made sense to me. The slinky is the best way I have ever been able to describe these things to people, especially with those who are not very spiritual or used to the New Age vernacular.

If you were to pull this slinky apart and stretch the rings to create more space, you would begin to see how the inner energetics can experience the cycles of *being*. The tighter you hold on internally, the tighter your slinky and the slower the growth. The more you learn to flow, the wider your slinky and the faster the growth. There are MANY people who have been holding on so tight that the moment they let go, their slinky is powerfully released.

The ability to stretch the space between the slinky cycles is governed by your own free will. The eternal truth is that you are always moving forward, but the energetic momentum of that process IS impacted by your free will (and your free will is about what is happening INSIDE you through the CHOICES you make). You are always in some way, shape, or form impacting the stretching in this never-ending slinky of *being*.

Whenever you are fighting the energies, you are pushing the slinky rings together and slowing down the growth process of your Soul. If your Soul growth was a movie, your free will is the remote controller that has the power either to slow down or speed up the process. There is no actual ability to stop or change the tape. Don't worry if this feels a bit weird. Just take what applies for you in this moment and work with it. We each have our unique perspective of the experience, and there are many perspectives to serve the many paths. The stretching of the slinky has to do with releasing your need to control (living from the Ego) and moving into a state of flow (living from the Soul).

The Sun in astrology represents this part of the individuated consciousness that is often referred to as the Ego.

Each year of your life, you will be inspired to take certain actions that are rooted in the I or the Ego. This is how your personality self grows, learns, and eventually awakens. You awaken first through the Ego and then move into an even more expanded knowing where you awaken to the Soul. Often, we get caught up with the Inner Speaker in our head and the chatter that it causes. Through the various roles and responsibilities we take on in our lives, our chatter box grows and, in many cases, takes on a mind of its own (feeling very disconnected from the Soul).

Each year when the Sun completes its circle, you are essentially at the new ring on your slinky. The Sun will move through the astrological houses yearly and continually activates the Ego to act and move forward. How you interact with the Ego and interpret the pulls and sensations within your life contributes to how your life unfolds (you have free will every step of the way). When we talk about stretching your slinky for more growth, clearly your "I" is a part of this process. If you are motivated to stretch that slinky (which I'm sure you are because I know I AM), then it is imperative to connect with the Sun in your yearly chart.

The Sun in your yearly chart will change positions in the astrological houses but ALWAYS remains in the exact same sign. I was born with the Sun at 3° Taurus, and every time the Sun is back at 3° Taurus, I'm one circle in my slinky further along. The same goes for you! This is because the slinky circle is complete only when the Sun makes its way back to its original starting point. The yearly chart is created based on this pattern, and this is exactly how it predicts the energy surrounding your year.

Since the Sun is always in the same degree and sign in your yearly chart, it is the astrological house that is of the greatest significance for interpretation. The house that gets activated by the Sun in the yearly chart indicates the area of your life that is ultimately up for review. When I say review, this is very important. I want you to imagine that in life there is the possibility of spiritual exams or even switching teachers. When the energy in a specific area of your life is up for review, it means you are going to be facing the decisions you have made in your life thus far and that you will have to determine what pivotal decisions you make next. Depending on the choices you make, you walk through a specific door. There are infinite choices and infinite doors. Alas, if you choose the same thing over and over again, you are choosing the same door as well (this is the karmic loop).

This karmic review often acts as a deep emotional trigger and forces you to make a choice.

This means if the Sun falls into your fourth house, which represents your home environment, you will feel called to review and evaluate that area of your life. This could surface in a multitude of ways but always centers on what the astrological house rules (and because of the complexity of astrology, each house rules a multitude of things). For instance, the fourth house rules home but also represents personal environment, ancestry, food, your mother, and real estate. Your spiritual review for the year is connected to the house where the Sun is located. During the year, you will often face important decisions (even if you don't consciously see them as such) around those specific areas of your life.

Here's the secret I want to tell you: Wherever the energy is blocked in your astrological house, that is what will be up for review. Let's explore each house to see what happens when the sun activates it in your yearly review.

Understanding what will energetically be surfacing for you throughout your year empowers you to make the best DECISION and CHOICE you can for yourself. As you are awakening first through your Ego, this can be very hard to navigate, and we are often led down many dead ends. Astrology lights the path and broadens your ability to understand and align with cosmos to support your growth. I always remind myself that our lives are composed of millions and millions of tiny choices AND that each of those choices matter greatly (no matter how small). You will be learning to identify the area of your life that is up for spiritual review so that you can consciously move forward on the most expansive path—and make the choices YOU truly want to make.

SPIRITUAL REVIEW
Houses Key for the Sun

House 1: Aries—The Warrior
Element: Fire
Areas up for Review: self, Ego, physical appearance, drive, approach to life, early childhood, personality, point of view

Active Energy Pull:
If the Sun is in your first house, there is most likely going to be a decision involving your physical appearance, physical health, or both. Your deeper need to express your individuality is being called to reflect in your physical body. This could be a moment of dramatic physical change in your life, such as losing 50 pounds, or this could be as simple as a change of hair color. The expression is unique to the life and circumstance but will always involve the physical body.

House 2: Taurus—The Builder
Element: Earth
Areas up for Review: finances, resources, values, money, investments, innate talents, movable property, possessions

Active Energy Pull:
If the Sun is in your second house, you will feel a new sense of independence when it comes to your finances. The common theme for you this year is financial independence. If you have been reliant on your parents, it may be time to step up and take over your own finances (cutting the financial umbilical cord once and for all). If you have been reliant on a spouse, you may feel an overwhelming urge to get a job and to start contributing financially for your family. On the flip side of this, if you have been responsible for paying another person's way to your own financial detriment, you are being called to take back control of your

own finances. No matter your circumstance, it is time to take control and to actively begin to secure or manage your own resources.

House 3: Gemini—The Storyteller
Element: Air
Areas up for Review: verbal communication, siblings, learning, short trips, sales, neighbors, early education, intelligence

Active Energy Pull:
If the Sun is in your third house, you are being called to communicate your needs with your friends, family, and siblings. This is an opportunity for you to truly learn how to use your voice to state your needs and boundaries. There can be a significant gray area when it comes to the responsibilities you feel toward your family and friends. Creating healthy boundaries is imperative to your life journey, and this lesson will be repeating itself until it is learned. IF you do not set healthy boundaries, you risk the possibility of becoming drained and deflated by the very relationships that should be supporting and elevating you to new heights.

House 4: Cancer—The Nurturer
Element: Water
Areas up for Review: private, personal comfort, family, ancestry, home, motherhood, real estate

Active Energy Pull:
If the Sun is in your fourth house, you may be moving or purchasing your first home. There is a new beginning for you in the area of personal, private, family, and home. If you have been dabbling with the idea of moving out of your current residence and perhaps living independently, the energy is now supporting this move. There is an overwhelming sense of freedom that will be achieved when you claim your power and choose where you want to live. There is certainly a shift in your home environment calling you that needs you to take action.

House 5: Leo—The Performer
Element: Fire
Areas up for Review: creative expression, children, romance, hobbies, fun, taking risks, pleasure, engagement, gambling

Active Energy Pull:

If the Sun is in the fifth house, this is a very significant year for you. Leo is the natural ruler of House 5, and this is a golden year, one where you will be able to shine brightly and express your inner creativity and love. All of the Leo characteristics are becoming activated within you this year; you are becoming more sociable, charming, and outgoing. You are able to make connections easily and create new and important relationships. This is a powerful time for you to tap into another facet of your personality. Be appreciative and humbled for these new gifts.

House 6: Virgo—The Craftsman
Element: Earth
Areas up for Review: daily habits, service to others, health, anxiety, pets, fitness, order, coworkers, routine, duty

Active Energy Pull:

If the Sun is in the sixth house, your health is of primary importance this year. There will be an overwhelming realization that your daily habits are impacting your health and well-being. If you have failed to maintain the health and integrity of your physical body, you may be burdened with illness or fatigue. This is not meant to set you back, but rather it is a wake-up call to you from Spirit. You can change, and this means that your circumstances can change as well. Clean eating and clean living are imperative to the function of your physical body. What you eat becomes your blood, your blood becomes your cells, and you are the composition of these cells. Make sure you are actively choosing how you treat your body from a conscious level.

House 7: Libra —The Peacemaker
Element: Air
Areas up for Review: relationships, one-on-one communication, legal matters, partnership, divorce, art, negotiations, contracts, agreements, lawsuits, open enemies, marriage

Active Energy Pull:
If the Sun is in the seventh house, there will be some dynamic shifts occurring in your relationships, and specifically your romantic relationships. You are filled with a sense of independence and are ready to express yourself and your needs. There can be a very great up-leveling that occurs in all or some of your relationships (both friendships and romantic relationships). Depending on your circumstances, this up-leveling may manifest as you choosing to end a relationship if it is no longer serving your highest good (or someone else taking the initiative to end a relationship). This is often a pivotal time when you are waking up to the choices you have made and deciding if they are in your best interest over the long haul.

House 8: Scorpio—The Alchemist
Element: Water
Areas up for Review: occult, endings, rebirth, wills/trusts, psychic powers, taxes, death, others moneys, sex, research

Active Energy Pull:
If the Sun is in the eighth house, there is some sort of ending and rebirth occurring in your life. On the physical level, this can be an indication that you will experience the passing of a relative or family pet. On the spiritual level, this can be an indication that you are walking away from a relationship or circumstance that was holding you back (often a relationship or circumstance that has been with you since childhood). This is a time of rebirth and can often be very emotional

as you work your way into a deeper understanding of self. As you experience this year, it is imperative that you remember that endings and new beginnings go hand in hand. Death is the karma of life, and life is the karma of death. Endings truly are always new beginnings.

House 9: Sagittarius—The Philosopher
Element: Fire
Areas up for Review: travel, writing, higher education, religion, philosophy, journey, exploration, publishing, literature

Active Energy Pull:
If the Sun is in the ninth house, this is a year of furthering your education, traveling, and expanding your mind. There will be plenty of opportunity for you this year to explore your more philosophical side. The hardest decision will be what direction you want to take! As you approach the opportunities you will receive this year, make sure that you are thinking long term and about the impact that this will have on your self-identity. This is a powerful time to return to schooling if the purpose is driven by a deeper sense and knowing (not related to making more money or feeding the lower self, which is guided only by desire). There is often an opportunity for foreign travel during this time, and you may even be inspired to travel by yourself for the first time in your life. Make sure that you take each of these moments and blessings in this year as one to be treasured.

House 10: Capricorn—The Entrepreneur
Element: Earth
Areas up for Review: career, life purpose, leadership, promotion, public eye, fame, career, authority, vocation, fatherhood, goals, reputation, social status

Active Energy Pull:

If the Sun is in the tenth house, your career is likely to hit a new high. You will be feeling like you can truly shine this year, and you will most likely receive a promotion or great praise and recognition for a job well done. You are feeling very driven this year to achieve your goals and to go after your dreams. This is very good energy for starting a new business or venture. You are self-assured and determined to make this year count in your life. The amount of energy you put back into any endeavor will most certainly be well nourished by the universal forces.

House 11: Aquarius—the Inventor
Element: Air
Areas up for Review: your social circle, innovation, movement forward, technology, collective vision, stepchildren, true self, destiny, friends, unexpected events

Active Energy Pull:

If the Sun is in the eleventh house, you are a leader among your peers. You have a new charismatic charm that is infectious. Friends and family are looking to spend time with you because of your new direction and confidence. This is a year when you feel appreciated by those around you and are feeling very generous with showing your affection and staying connected to those who matter to you. Use this opportunity to continue to build on these connections and to branch out and meet new people. There is great potential to make very powerful friendships during this time. You will naturally step into the role of the teacher and begin to cultivate relationships where you act as a mentor.

House 12: Pisces—The Artist
Element: Water
Areas up for Review: religion, dreams, hidden enemies, addictions, karma, support, faith, unconscious, escapism, fear, healing support, hidden talents

Active Energy Pull:

If the Sun is in the twelfth house, you have a year that is emphasizing your spiritual growth and supporting you in opening to new beliefs. Through spirituality and religion, we are often able to open ourselves up to the grand scheme or the larger universal design. It's years like these that will lead you to the big and important questions. This can be scary at times because you will be wanting answers and may not know where to turn. Looking to others for guidance, reading books, taking classes, and absorbing yourself in the arts are very good ways to stretch your perspective. The only caveat is that the ultimate answers are always within you. Seek to always keep your own guidance as you embrace and integrate what speaks to your truth on your path.

Vision Sheet Instructions
Discovering the Energetic Review for Your Year

STEP I:

Look to table 1, columns 1 and 4, of your Cosmic Navigator to determine the Annual house location of the Sun. This will tell you the house location of the Sun, which changes yearly and where the spiritual review will take place.

Part 1:

On the front page of your Vision Sheet, there is a giant circle in the middle that is an astrological chart, and the 12 segments correspond to the 12 astrological houses. Each of the house numbers is written into the outer segment of the circle; the numbers are 1–12 and move sequentially in a counterclockwise pattern around the chart. You will need to locate the house number that you determined above and write "Sun—Spiritual Review" into the appropriate segment. You can enter it into the outer part of the circle (see example Vision Sheet for reference if needed).

STEP 2:

Now that you have identified the house, it's time to learn about the areas of the life that the house rules, and read about what area of your life is up for review on page 42.

STEP 3:

There are two important parts to this work: knowing the areas of life up for review and understanding where you will most likely be seeing the most amount of change during your year. Together we will work to see the pattern and prepare you to make the most out of your year.

Part 1:

After you have read about the areas of life that are ruled by the astrological house where your Sun is located, I want you to take a minute to connect in deeply with yourself. Ask yourself: In what area do I feel the energy flows the slowest or may be wanting support? What stood out and felt very clear to me? Is there an emotional block that I should be aware of?

Part 2:

This is very, very important. Please take your time and record whatever is coming to you now in the Insights box on the back of the Vision Sheet. I will remind you often on this journey that the work you are doing now with this Vision Sheet is about supporting you later. Add all of your insights, including where you believe you may have an emotional block to support you as the year unfolds. You can label this insight "Insight #2: Spiritual Review."

V

Your Energetic Approach to the Year

←——————————————————→

It is clear that the world is on the brink of greatness or destruction, and the energy that is held within the individual is the determining factor. Do we continue to fear each other and create violence masked as self-defense? Or do we embrace our birthright and the truth that we are spiritual beings originating from the same source? We have a choice to make: Either lean into each other through connection, or lean away from each other in destruction. There are two primary forces in the world—fear and love—and we get to decide the path we take.

When I first started doing readings for friends, it was always supportive and enlightening but tended to lack a certain power. It wasn't until I started doing readings for complete strangers that I truly discovered the power of astrology. The true gift of astrology is that it knows the unknowable. And to know the unknowable creates certain implications, energetic movement, and awakening within the Soul. When the Soul has been seen, understood, and truly reflected, there is a moment of Soul recognition, acceptance, and validation. This is because the most important question has finally been answered: You most certainly are Spirit in a human body.

If you were not, how could astrology know the unknowable?

You receive physical traits from your physical parents. You receive energetic traits from your spiritual parents. These energy parents are the 12 signs of the zodiac. For instance, you may have a lot of Aries (The Warrior) energy in this lifetime because you inherited a dominant amount of those traits from your spiritual parent known as Aries (The Warrior). I have a ton of Taurus (The Builder) in my chart, and I have inherited many spiritual traits from my spiritual parent, Taurus (The Builder). Each of us displays various energetic tendencies and patterns due to the amount of the signs that we inherit in each lifetime.

That being said, just because we have dominant energy within the 12 signs doesn't mean we are without the traits from the other signs. All 12 signs are within us at varying degrees, and although we will show an affinity to certain tendencies, the goal is to mature our usage of ALL the signs. This is about harmonizing, finding balance, and learning how to choose to align with ALL the traits of the 12 signs.

There have been times in my life when I have had to call upon the energy of one of the 12 signs that is not apparent in my birth chart. There will always be times for the boldness and passion of Aries, and equally there are times for the skepticism and critical thought of Scorpio. My dominant Taurus energy has also created certain limiting energetics that I have had to move beyond as well.

Each year of your life you are being influenced by one of these 12 signs to grow, mature, and embrace its qualities. Essentially, you are activated to approach the year with a new energetic outlook (you will have felt this at various points in your life). Some years you've wanted to make big changes, and other years you've wanted to lie low. Those influences you naturally took on are a reflection of how the signs change your approach to life yearly.

If you remember as a little child, you would reach out to hold someone's hand as you crossed the road to guide you. Each year, one of the 12 spiritual parents reaches out to guide you. It ignites that energetic force within you and allows you to tap into the power it holds. This is why I love astrology—because it knows the unknowable that you already know inside. The mind can't deny the truth, and because of this, it gets to step out of linear thinking (if only for a few minutes).

What is known as the Ascendant or Rising Sign in your yearly chart reflects the energetic approach you will take to your year. This is the energy of the spiritual parent that is reaching out to take your hand and guide you! You literally get to see if you are meant to approach the year as The Warrior or The Peacemaker. I suspect, however, that you already have awareness of this inner pull.

Before we deeply explore the Ascendant in your yearly chart, we need to tap back into the energy of the Sun in your birth chart. This is because this is the expression that remains constant throughout your life. I want you to keep this in the back of your mind as you explore your approach to the year. You will find that this will broaden your perspective and allow you to connect the dots. Someone who has a core lesson of FIRE will not react exactly the same when they have a yearly approach with that same element as someone who does not. This is the same concept as how someone would approach yoga who has never done it before, versus someone who has been doing it for years. Due to their experience and understanding, the experience is altered accordingly.

Don't worry if you are a little confused right now. Just focus on what you are about to read relating to your core lesson based on your Sun sign through the text below.

Most people know their Sun Sign by heart, and it is this sign we are exploring from a new lens right now (this sign remains the same both in the natal/birth chart and the yearly chart and is highly significant to your development of Self). Below, the Sun Signs have been separated into their Elements: Fire, Earth, Air, Water. Right now we are exploring the core lesson of each element so that you can understand the significance of the integration of the Ascendant/Rising Sign energy in your yearly chart. Take a moment now to locate your sign below and identify the element. Once you locate it, read on to learn more about your core lesson.

FIRE: ARIES, LEO, SAGITTARIUS

The Fire element is notorious for its intellectual swiftness and ability to take action. This is a very powerful energy that is infectious and often found in charismatic leaders. What the Fire element lacks is the ability to see projects through to fruition (and also a tendency to become short tempered and aggressive in the process). In order to ground this energy, Fire must learn how to control its abundant passion and find ways to bring it down to earth.

When things don't go right with their endeavors/pursuits immediately, there is an automatic response for the fire element to jump ship. While there are definitely times when this is the appropriate action to take, the Fire element dances with the issue of doing this too soon and too often. When this comes to important endeavors/relationships, the Fire element then suffers because they struggle to reach the stage of fruition.

The first step is creating space around the central issue and learning to take a step back versus jumping ship or taking dramatic action. When that adrenaline kicks in (and it always does), you must find a different outlet to release the fire you feel within. This outlet is typically physical exercise but can be whatever you choose to release the steam and heat. This will help shift your awareness and bring an objective nature to the issue at hand. Practice waiting 24 hours before taking immediate action whenever you can (and please note, you almost always can). It will take some practice for you to get comfortable with this new approach, but it will serve you very well throughout your life journey.

When Fire learns this valuable lesson and begins to slow down, their results will actually begin to speed up. This will create room for the Fire element to learn to view objectively and to realize that the "do or die" energy is just the passionate flame that is blazing in their heart.

EARTH: TAURUS, VIRGO, CAPRICORN

The Earth element is very practical, grounded, and dedicated to the work they have set out to do. There is a fierce loyalty inherent to this element and a powerful ability to commit. With this strength comes the greatest weakness of the Earth element: an inability to walk away when something is not truly serving their highest good. This element often confuses consciously walking away from endeavors with the same energy of quitting. Since this energy cannot stomach the idea of quitting and giving up, the lesson that is deeply needed within this energy is to learn how to release and let go.

Due to the nature of this sign sticking to endeavors/relationships that no longer serve their highest good, they often create circumstances that force those specific issues/relationships to come to a dramatic ending or turning point. These turning points are often very hard on the Earth energy due to their inherent sense of obligation to behave at their very best and succeed. Confusingly, the lesson to be learned is not necessarily about the situation that came to a head. The true lesson that the Earth element needs to learn is to listen to their internal knowing.

When something feels off, the Earth signs automatically go into the mode of cultivation, meaning they immediately start to "work" and tend to the situation. This is because they are master cultivators, and many times they can use this skill to get the relationship/endeavor back to where they "believe" in their heart it belongs. This is a noble pursuit for short periods of time, but the Earth sign will inevitably have to learn to walk away (because not everyone or everything is meant for the long term).

An easy rule of thumb for this energy is to follow the "21 day" rule and understand its practical application. It takes us roughly 21 days to form a new habit. This indicates that if the cultivation the Earth energy has infused into their endeavor/relationship has not made an impact in this time frame, it probably will have no more success doing so beyond this. Once the Earth element learns to let go and honor that they don't need to stay in a constant state of cultivation, then life will stop behaving in a way that brings them unnecessary drama.

Air: Gemini, Libra, Aquarius

The Air element has a powerful gift of seeing the big picture coupled with a very strong intellect that focuses on creating solutions. This is a puzzle-solving element, and there is a constant desire to discuss, debate, and find solutions to virtually any problem. Because the Air element can easily detach emotionally, it often gets stuck in its own head. The lesson to be learned by this element is how to discover the on/off switch for their miraculous and uncanny ability for intense thinking.

The Air element is always on a mission to solve a problem, and due to their nature to serve the collective, they truly are focused on issues that matter. This is why the Air element struggles to manage their internal thinker; they love to think about what they are thinking about. When this happens, it becomes almost impossible for this element to disconnect from their pursuit. It is not so much that the Air element itself feels uncomfortable about their obsessive thinking, but the issue arises when this negatively impacts the relationships that they hold dear.

There is a deep need to learn how to turn this skill of thinking on and off so that the Air element can connect with others (and catch a much-needed break). This element can easily get lost in their mind, making them forget all the amazing things that are surrounding them in the physical world. One of the steps I recommend is to specifically schedule time to take off from their work or thinking. Typically, this involves a physical disconnection from computers, televisions, and cellular phones (because the Air energy tends to become addicted to these sorts of things).

The Air element is drawn to technology and communication. When they consciously choose to shut off and power down the specific devices they have grown accustomed to interacting with, something incredible will begin to occur. This forces the shifting of their energy into the present and the physical environment (the very thing their loved ones have probably been nagging them about). Now they can move away from being engaged with the thinker and can engage with their physical environment. When Air learns to let go of always being in the thinking mind, they will ironically find many of the solutions that had evaded them.

WATER: CANCER, SCORPIO, PISCES

The Water element is highly psychic, intuitive, and empathetic. The emotional intelligence of this element is untouched by the other elements in the zodiac. With this constant desire to connect and use its emotional intelligence to help others, the Water element forgets about the most important person of all, themselves.

The Water element needs to learn how to create boundaries and a separation of self from others. This is a lesson that is often learned through their relationships, and it expresses in all types: romantic, friendships, family, and work. The lesson of boundaries they are learning is very valuable and also evasive to them. This is because we are all connected and Water feels this spiritual truth deeply. Despite this truth, Water faces a conundrum—when operating in the Earth plane we are also separate, focused on cultivating an awareness of our own individuality. The lesson for Water is to learn how to create boundary lines for themselves (because it is too easy to feed into the energy of others and get lost due to their psychic nature).

My top recommendation for working with this lesson is to create a red flag or boundary list. This means you will have to sit down and create a very specific guideline for yourself, and then, of course, you will also have to follow it. This should be specific and be something that will support you in making those new choices that will open new doors.

Vision Sheet Instructions

UΠDERSTAΠDIΠG YOUR YEARLY APPROACH AΠD CREATIΠG YOUR PERSOΠAL MAΠTRA

You now have a good sense of the lesson and dynamic present in your Sun Sign based on element. This is a lesson that gets repeated over and over again throughout your life. The exploration we are doing now is to see what sign you are integrating into your approach. Keep this bigger lesson in the back of your mind as we embark on discovering how you will be approaching your year.

STEP 1:

It's time to connect with this energy! Look to table 1, columns 1 and 2, of your Cosmic Navigator to determine the Ascendant (a.k.a. Rising Sign) in your yearly chart. You will find the Ascendant listed under "Sensitive Points" in table 1, column 1. The sign of the Ascendant is listed in column 2 and represents your energetic approach to the year. Now that you have determined the sign of the Ascendant, you will read more about its impact on page 63. Once you have read this information, you will proceed to step 2.

STEP 2:

Each of the signs has a set of archetypes that represent the energy of the sign. Reread the list of archetypes with your Rising Sign and take a moment to feel which archetype resonates with you. Once you have selected it, enter the archetype into the blank circle in the middle of the Vision Sheet under the space where you wrote in the date of the year. For example, if I am exploring 2017–2018 and have Leo Rising, I will write in the archetype that I resonate with the most below the date. In this case, I chose "The Magical Child."

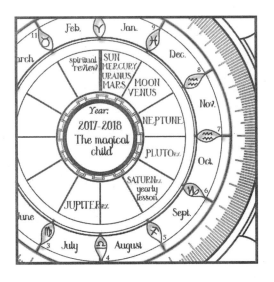

STEP 3:

It's now time for you to create your yearly mantra. One of the most powerful ways for you to align with this energy throughout the year is to create a shortcut. To do this, you will be creating your very own yearly mantra, and I will be guiding you through the process. It's important that YOU create the mantra because it must have specific importance to you and your life.

Part 1:

Each sign has a personal power phrase associated with its energy. At the top of your Vision Sheet, there is a row of 12 rectangles that correlate with the 12 signs of the zodiac. Use the key that follows to look up the Ascendant sign and identify the personal power phrase. Once you have it, you can write it in the rectangle just below the appropriate zodiac sign at the top of your Vision Sheet. For example, if you have Leo (The Performer) as your Ascendant, you would write I WILL in the blank lower square. Go ahead and take a minute to connect with this energy and make sure to write your yearly power phrase.

Power Phrase Key

Sign	Power Phrase
Aries	I AM
Taurus	I HAVE
Gemini	I THINK
Cancer	I FEEL
Leo	I WILL
Virgo	I ANALYZE
Libra	I BALANCE
Scorpio	I DESIRE
Sagittarius	I AIM
Capricorn	I UTILIZE
Aquarius	I KNOW
Pisces	I BELIEVE

STEP 4:

Once you have taken a moment to digest this information, you will create a one-sentence mantra for your year. There are two ways to do this: freestyle or guided (you will select the option below). Feel free to read through both methods to choose which one feels right for you. Once again, it may seem like creating a mantra right now will slow you down, but you have to trust me. These actions you take right **now** are the very thing you will be thankful for **later**.

Once you have this completed, you will record your final personal mantra under the "Insights" portion of the Vision Sheet and can label it as "Insight #3: Personal Mantra."

Freestyle Personal Mantra

STEP 1:

You will create a short personal mantra to embrace and encourage yourself to integrate the energy of the sign on your Ascendant. All of this is connected to the information you read in this specific chapter. There are only three rules to creating your mantra:

1. It must include the personal power phrase of the sign.
2. You must also include your selected archetype for the sign.
3. It must feel good and inspiring to you when you say it.

Note: You may want to reread the description of the sign energy one more time before creating your personal mantra.

Guided Personal Mantra

If you would like additional guidance to support you in completing your personal mantra, please follow the instructions below.

STEP 1:

Grab a piece of scrap paper so that you can easily work out the mantra and revise it until it is workable.

STEP 2:

Fold the paper lengthwise and, on the left-hand side, write down the personal power phrase you identified in step 1. For example, Leo is "I WILL."

STEP 3:

On the right-hand side, write down the archetype that you selected. For example, the archetype selected for Leo is "The Magical Child."

STEP 4:

You will need to energetically create some space and allow yourself to resonate with these words. Here is the most powerful question you can ask yourself right now: Why did you choose the archetype that you selected?

I have found that people do one of two things: They select the archetype they most closely view themselves as, OR they select the archetype that has traits they would like to have or feel they lack. Once you have identified your WHY, then you can create your mantra from a heightened perspective to support that deeper intention that you most likely weren't aware of.

STEP 5:

Trust yourself. This is imperative because the mantra is for you and written by YOU. This is about tapping into the larger part of your being and creating a shortcut back to this space throughout your entire year. Below are some examples to support you, but I must stress that this is not about taking a mantra somebody else has created (because it just doesn't work the same energetically).

EXAMPLE: LEO RISING/THE MAGICAL CHILD
I WILL embrace the magical child within by having fun, laughing, playing, and leading.

EXAMPLE: ARIES RISING/THE WARRIOR
I AM a Warrior of light, and I'm not afraid to shine and be who I am.

EXAMPLE: GEMINI RISING/THE STORYTELLER
I THINK and use my Storyteller to share stories, connect, and build new relationships.

Bonus! For Those Who Have Read *Claiming Your Power*!

If you have already completed my first book, *Claiming Your Power Through Astrology*, I encourage you to complete this bonus section to build on the insights you've discovered working with astrology. We are going to move into a slightly advanced astrological concept, linking your yearly/annual chart back to your birth chart for extremely important information. **This has been said to be one of the most powerful approaches to interpreting the yearly chart and HOW it allows you to manifest the potential in your birth chart.**

STEP 1:

In table 1, columns 1 and 5, you will look up the location of your yearly Ascendant to see the house location it takes in the astrological houses of your birth chart. First locate the "Ascendant" under "Sensitive Points" and then scroll to the column labeled "Natal House."

STEP 2:

Once you determine the house location, you have discovered the area of your birth chart that is being brought to life throughout the year. This is the lock and key for how the yearly chart connects back in with your birth chart (potential for the life). It is not a simple interpretation, but an important one. To understand the significance of the house activated, you have to have a full understanding of that house in your birth chart.

Part 1:

In chapter 1 of *Claiming Your Power*, look to the second worksheet: House Exploration. Now that you know the House that your yearly ascendant falls into, you can see exactly what area of your birth chart is being stimulated to GROW. This is as if you are shining a light onto the potential locked within that house of your birth chart.

Part 2:

Check out the activity going on in that house in your birth chart to get an idea of how this will be unfolding for you. (You may even want to look through all of your completed worksheets from that book to really dive deep.) If there were a lot of planets in that birth chart house, you have a lot of energetic potential and innate talents to be worked with throughout your year. Take a moment to record your insights or "aha's" into the Insights section on the back side of your Vision Sheet.

YEARLY APPROACH
Exploring the Ascendant (a.k.a. Rising Sign)

Aries: The Warrior

Archetypes: The Warrior, The Leader, The Dare-Devil, The Pioneer, The Champion

Personal Power Phrase: I AM

Aries is a sign of passion, creativity, and leadership. As the first sign in the zodiac, it is apparent that this is an initiating energy that gets the ball rolling. When Aries is taking your hand and guiding you to approach life with its vitality, you are being called to stand up and consciously choose your path. This is about trusting your instincts, pursuing your passion, and choosing to be bold. This may or may not come easy for you, depending on the energy of your birth chart. If you are someone who fears taking the lead or making big decisions, this year could potentially feel heavy and force you to break some repeated patterns. This is about stepping into the energy of The Warrior, building your confidence, and moving down your path in the way that you truly desire. For those who already demonstrate the qualities of Aries, be forewarned not to trample people as you excitedly align with this pull. Aries may be The Warrior, but as you grow in awareness you realize that it is the Peaceful Warrior that brings about the change we all truly desire.

TAURUS: THE BUILDER

ARCHETYPES: THE BUILDER, THE STABILIZER, THE ECONOMIZER, THE PROVIDER, THE NATURE ARTIST

PERSONAL POWER PHRASE: I HAVE

Taurus is a sign of responsibility, resourcefulness, and fully committing. This is the energy that fuels the seed to move from a tiny seedling to a gigantic oak tree. Do not underestimate the power of The Builder and what it will support you in accomplishing. This energy will ask you to fully commit, move forward, and take the good with the bad. Often we become obsessed with what is good for us in the short term and miss out on the gifts that are the fruit of longer labors. This year you should consider what you are wanting to experience over the long term and what actionable steps you will need to take. The resourcefulness of this energy will help you see the way and will call to you the right people, events, and circumstances to begin to harness this energy. Most people overestimate what they can accomplish in one year and underestimate what they can accomplish in a decade. Taurus wants you to think about things from a new vantage point that is more concerned with what you can do in a decade versus what you can do in a year. The trick of this is that each decade is simply 10 years: When you live all of those years completely, you accomplish EXACTLY what you set out to accomplish for the decade.

GEMINI: THE STORYTELLER

ARCHETYPES: THE STORYTELLER, THE COMMUNICATOR, THE LEADER, THE TEACHER, THE TRICKSTER

PERSONAL POWER PHRASE: I THINK

Gemini is a fun-loving, tenacious, charming energy that is excitable and quick to change its mind. This year is about having fun, connecting through conversation, and trying out new things. Gemini gives you permission to try out new things and actually encourages you to change your mind if that is the truth within you! So often we get stuck in doing the same old thing. The older you become, the harder it becomes to break those patterns. This is because the unknown always causes more fear than the known. The older we get, the less used to that feeling we have, and so we unconsciously try to avoid it! Don't believe me? The 23-year-old out of college faces less fear on their first day on the job than the 50-year-old who is switching careers after 25 years doing the same thing. Why? Repeated patterns provide a form of comfort (even if you don't like the repeated pattern you are in!).

You have to be brave, step out of your comfort zone, and try new things. Gemini learned long ago that the path to enlightenment requires you to make choices. Every day you choose. Choosing to stick with something is just as much of a choice as choosing to move on to the next thing. If you ever feel like the rest of your life is a known story and that you probably won't have any more surprises, Gemini urges you to deeply question yourself and your choices! When you play it safe, you don't always grow to your full potential. All of your growth happens outside your comfort zone, and Gemini knows this and loves this. It is an energy that wants you to grow, change, adapt, and become whatever it is you want to be (and this of course changes throughout your life).

Cancer: The Nurturer

Archetypes: The Nurturer, The Preserver, The Counselor, The Healer, The Protector

Personal Power Phrase: I FEEL

With Cancer Rising you are stepping deeper into your emotions and learning how to let people in. Cancer is represented by the crab, and this symbol represents our tendency to retreat in the face of danger (even if the danger is an illusion of the mind). This is a year when you are looking straight at the core of your being and deciding to retreat or move forward. You may feel much more sensitive to your environment. Even if you had always had a thick skin, you may feel as if things are now getting beyond your outer wall (and there is nothing you can do to stop it).

The energy of Cancer tends to hang on to things, both physically and emotionally. This energy to not let go can be helpful for those who move too fast and do not stick with things. Keep in mind that if you already have the tendency to hang on and not let go, you'll have to keep an eye on that. Feeling deeply is a part of how we learn to guide ourselves, but we have to develop a way to interpret, understand, express, and then release the emotions as they arise. Allow this year to stretch you and focus on being aware of your deeper feelings. It is okay if you consciously choose to retreat from a situation like the crab, but let that be a decision that comes from the right place.

LEO: THE PERFORMER

ARCHETYPES: THE PERFORMER, THE ACTOR, THE CLOWN, THE MAGICAL CHILD, THE LEADER

PERSONAL POWER PHRASE: I WILL

Leo is the energy of the performer and is full of creativity, passion, and a childlike hunger to experience the world. There is always a playfulness to this energy that is positive, upbeat, and fearless. This year, Leo teaches you to let go, have fun, and allow the child in you to come out and play. With all the responsibilities of life, there can be times when we forget to literally be happy and enjoy our lives. We focus so hard on attaining things that we don't even take the time to appreciate and be with the things we have. Take a look around the room you are sitting in and digest what you see. Are you taking care of, enjoying, and making use of all the things you have? One of my favorite ways of realizing this insight is through children. It is always wonderful to see a child transform the common item in the home to their most favorite toy. You could buy them hundreds of gadgets, but those gadgets can't compete with the simple act of the water running out of a faucet. Be grateful for what you have and be sure to enjoy it with new perspective.

VIRGO: THE CRAFTSMAN

ARCHETYPES: THE CRAFTSMAN, THE EXAMINER, THE EDITOR, THE MENTOR, THE WISE MASTER

PERSONAL POWER PHRASE: I ANALYZE

The energy of Virgo is a very significant energy in the zodiac because it encompasses all five signs before it. It is the turning point in the zodiac where the energy moves from an individual orientation to a community orientation. In fact, Virgo is the energy that has one foot on each side. It understands the importance of individuality and community equally and always strives to bring harmony to this process.

There is a keen sense of awareness about how things function, a hunger to make things function as best as they can, and the ability to take things to the next level. This year you will be assessing virtually everything in your life, and this is not because you are being overly critical or are having a midlife crisis (although I can't say with certainty that you are not). The want to evaluate is natural to this sign, and you will want to look back on the life you have created. Now you get to check back in with yourself to ensure that your path is unfolding the way that you truly want. This is one of the smartest things you could do (and Virgo is beyond smart). Allow yourself to disconnect so that you can reconnect from a new, broader perspective. You will be very thankful that you did.

LIBRA: THE PEACEMAKER

ARCHETYPES: THE PEACEMAKER, THE DIPLOMAT, THE STRATEGIST, THE COMPANION, THE FINE ARTIST

PERSONAL POWER PHRASE: I BALANCE

Libra is a harmonizing energy that has the tendency to always see both sides, seek beauty, and do anything within its power to continually avoid facing conflict. This year will have a lighter feeling within as you align with the weightless Air energy of Libra. You will be floating through the year with an ability to see both the good and the bad, and a deep desire to chose to see the beauty within. Be aware of avoiding decisions as you begin to see in shades of gray.

Libra is known as the great balancer, and although it is The Peacemaker, it isn't afraid to bring things back into balance if need be. Libra is the energy that, once the chaos level hits a breaking point, will speak up and take charge. As you go through the year, remember to ask yourself: Am I truly keeping balance in my life? Has work become all that I have time for? Am I so wrapped up in a pursuit that I have lost touch with other areas of my life that truly inspire me? When is the last time I had a home-cooked meal and truly nourished my body? There is always a balancing act taking place within that works to harmonize the mind, body, and spirit. This year Libra takes your hand and brings these three aspects of self back into balance: mind, body, and spirit. Depending on how you have been balancing these aspects on your own, Libra may need to snap you back into a place of balance (this can feel intense if you have been deeply out of balance). This is Libra's job after all, and all you need to do is trust it and strive to keep the balance.

Scorpio: The Alchemist

Archetypes: The Alchemist, The Detective, The Manager, The Researcher, The Investigator

Personal Power Phrase: I DESIRE

There is no sign in the zodiac as misunderstood and judged as Scorpio. This is of course because it is a very powerful energy that is impossible for others to control. Scorpio represents both the scorpion and the eagle, reflecting the grand-scale growth you achieve during your earthly incarnations. It's about moving from actions taken in fear through the Small Self, all the way to actions taken in love through the Higher Self.

You will begin to sense the importance and power of this year and YOUR ability to influence how the path unfolds. You will constantly need to ask yourself: Is this action being taken due to inner fear? Or is this action being taken due to inner love? Every action taken in fear will bring more fear. Every action taken in love will bring more love. This is the year when you get to see just how far you've come and where you are at. With this energetic power, you can at times feel on top of the world. The misstep often taken here is to give in to the Ego demands and focus on the material world. The other mistake is in giving in to the False Messiah and falling prey to desire for power. Never forget that what you leave with at the end of your life is what truly counts. It is the experiences and the love in your heart for yourself and others that support you once you leave.

Sagittarius: The Philosopher

Archetypes: The Philosopher, The Seeker, The Explorer, The Gypsy, The Teacher

Personal Power Phrase: I Aim

The energy of Sagittarius will have you thinking, pondering, plotting, and getting ready for some sort of adventure or new experience. This could be returning to school, going on a trip, or reading more books in one year than you have in a decade. That is the energy of this sign, and it is hungry to learn, experience, and grow.

There is a charismatic charm to this energy, but it often forgets its responsibilities as it goes on this wild ride. This year is about taking the adventure without having to take the fall after it's over. Can you ground in your roots and ensure that the adventure you want is taken from a responsible place? If you don't, you will still experience that beautiful high, but you will also have some sort of repercussion if you go about it haphazardly and don't plan for its execution. There is always a way to bring that sense of adventure for the short term without letting it take you over and derail your long-term goals. This year you'll find out how well you've gotten at working with this energy.

CAPRICORN: THE ENTREPRENEUR

ARCHETYPES: THE ENTREPRENEUR, THE EXECUTIVE, THE AUTHORITY, THE MANAGER, THE ADVISOR

PERSONAL POWER PHRASE: I UTILIZE

The Capricorn energy is the energy of the commander, war chief, entrepreneur, and old soul. It has ambitious goals it wants to achieve, and it is happy to take its time. There will be a methodical approach to the year that is well thought out and strategic. This can be the moment you begin your journey for a long-term goal you set or when you finally achieve what was set into motion years ago.

The truth of this energy is that the true experience NEVER happens in the attaining of the goal. The least exciting part of the journey is when it ends. How do we know this? Because once you arrive at any goal, within hours you are ready to set out on an even-bigger journey. Once you begin to see this pattern, you will transcend that restless need of the Ego to attain and shift into the whole energy of the Spirit that is to experience. Use this year to bring yourself back to this simple core truth and seek peace and wholeness as you take your next steps forward.

Aquarius: The Inventor

Archetypes: The Inventor, The Innovator, The Reformer, The Humanitarian, The Cosmic Genius

Personal Power Phrase: I Know

With Aquarius rising on the eastern horizon of your yearly chart, you are embracing all the wonderful traits of this powerful sign. Knowing that you are in the Age of Aquarius adds to the power of this year because you are very much a changemaker during this year of your life. Aquarius is an Air sign and has a heightened perspective of all that it sees. It seeks the big patterns, the grand design, and to simply know for the power of knowing.

You will be obsessed with finding a solution to a problem during this year of your life. It could present as many little problems or one big problem, but your energy will be shifting to finding the solution rather than dwelling in circumstance. That means that if you're in a horrible amount of debt, this is the year you seek the solution and begin to change the pattern that caused that circumstance. Or if you are stuck in an addiction, this is the year when you begin to want to change that circumstance and find a new way. The energy of Aquarius has a unique way of removing enough of the stuck emotional nature to support in changing what IS. Since you will be prone to getting sucked into your own world this year, keep awareness around your relationships. This behavior is often misinterpreted and experienced as you becoming detached or not interested. Let people know what is going on with you, and prevent this common misunderstanding.

PISCES: THE ARTIST

ARCHETYPES: THE ARTIST, THE HEALER, THE DREAMER, THE POET, THE VISIONARY ARTIST

PERSONAL POWER PHRASE: I BELIEVE

The Pisces energy will begin to soften you in a very unique way that actually strengthens you in the long run. The paradoxical nature of our universe is that what is soft is actually strong. Those who are flexible and release the need to control bend with the wind and don't break when the storm blows through. Pisces is the final sign within the zodiac, and it embraces a little bit of the 11 signs that precede it. That means that there are many expressions and rays of this sign that will be pulsating through you during this year. The beauty of Pisces is that it has an earnest need to serve and help others in an expressive way. It understands the deeper need of humanity to feel seen, heard, and understood.

This year is about listening and not talking as much. Take time to release your need to control, offer advice, and act by using force to make yourself heard. The inner part of you that wants to be seen and understood exists in every single one of us. To hear and understand another is paradoxically the only way that you can be heard and understood. When we allow the individual nature of our being to lose its tight grip on how we behave, we shift into a more expansive space of awareness and acceptance. It is only from a space of learning to find yourself in others that you can truly be found.

CHAPTER SIX

The Collective Energy Cycle

As all of these powerful aspects of your year are coming into light, it's important to take a moment to recognize that although we are individual beings, we all exist within a much-larger community of consciousness—that community of consciousness is called humanity. We are deeply connected to each other, our planet, and our solar system (the Milky Way galaxy). Because of this deep connection, we all experience the collective energy, but it is so deeply ingrained in us that we often miss it or are unaware that it exists.

Think of how you are literally on the Earth, but you can't actually feel it moving through space or rotating on its axis. This is something that you are experiencing 24 hours a day, seven days a week, for your whole lifetime, and you cannot actually feel that movement. That's because you are a part of that movement, and it is in you and happening through you. We all are literally moving through space together.

These collective energy cycles are very real, and once you gain awareness of these cycles, you will be shocked at how we unknowingly are influenced to take action in alignment with them. This information will allow you to have a powerful awareness of the world around you, the behaviors you're seeing in others, and how the collective is growing and developing throughout your year. Just as we grow and develop as individuals, the collective does as well (and the collective needs us to support, nurture, and understand the very important growth stages it is in). I believe if you are reading this book, you have the ability to serve the collective and stretch that collective slinky! You are a person who is here to ignite the changes of these cycles and pave the way. This information is vital in allowing us to rise to the potential of our lives as we are deeply connected to team humanity.

Astrological Ages

My first introduction to the astrological ages was the song "Age of Aquarius," and I'm sure for many of you reading this book, you discovered the existence of astrological ages in a similar way. Although it was catchy and I knew that it sounded mystical and intriguing, I hadn't a clue as to what it meant or its significance. It wasn't until I had my lesson on the astrological ages that I realized the importance of this aspect of astrology. It is safe to say that I was mesmerized. My mentor Nancy led me through history with the astrological ages as the backdrop, and it all finally made sense. The Age of Cancer (water sign) coincided with Noah and the great flood; The Age of Taurus (earth sign), with the birth of agriculture. So forth and so on, insight after insight.

Astrology has long been dedicated to understanding the broader growth patterns of the collective. You may have heard of what is called the precession of the equinoxes at some point on your journey, but often it isn't fully explained (or understood). The precession of the equinoxes is a very important cycle that is known as the Great Year. Due to gravity, the Earth has a wobble that reminds me very much of a dreidel when it is spinning and begins to lose momentum. This axial rotation creates a cycle of the Earth's movement, which lasts 26,000 years (this is what causes the precession of the equinoxes). Through this process, the 0° Aries in the tropical zodiac technically falls backward through the constellation of stars.

This rotation that lasts 26,000 years, the Great Year, is very significant to us spiritually and collectively. The Great Year is broken up by the 12 signs of the zodiac into what are called ages. We go through all the ages in a rhythmic pattern, integrating the energy of the sign into the collective and growing together. Although the human life span does not last an entire astrological age, we the collective (community of consciousness) continue to work through the energy of all 12 signs. Each of these ages lasts for roughly 2,166 years (26,000 years in a Great Year; 12 signs = 2,166 years per sign). This is what is being referred to when people say we are entering the Age of Aquarius. We are currently beginning the process of moving the energy through the collective that aligns with the great power of Aquarius, The Inventor.

In astrology, the planets are always moving forward through the zodiac in the following order: Aries, Taurus, Gemini, Cancer, Leo, Virgo, Libra, Scorpio, Sagittarius, Capricorn, Aquarius, and Pisces. The only exception to that rule is when a planet is retrograde and appears to be moving backward. Retrograde is an optical illusion of the planet moving backward due to the geocentric nature of astrology (focusing on the movement of planets as viewed from the Earth). No planet actually ever stops the direction it is moving in or turns around.

When it comes to the Great Year, the movement is actually falling backward through the zodiac. This means the Great Year has the opposite flow through the zodiac: Pisces, Aquarius, Capricorn, Sagittarius, Scorpio, Libra, Virgo, Leo, Cancer, Gemini, Taurus, and Aries. It is called the precession of the equinoxes because it is at the spring equinox when the 0° Aries that aligns with the constellation every 26,000 years begins to slip backward. As we enter each of the ages, we bring deeper integration of that particular sign into the collective. This falling back is what has confused many people when it comes to astrology and Sun signs (because the Tropical Zodiac doesn't match up with the constellations consistently). Without going into the rabbit hole on this, the Tropical Zodiac focuses on the seasonal changes, and it is known that 0° Aries lines up with the constellation roughly every 26,000 years or so. In addition to this, the physical constellations are of varying sizes (not each 30°), and therefore there is no match-up for the zodiac signs when they are 30° anyway.

The tropical zodiac approaches these energetic forces through different mathematics and is based on the four major turning points of the Earth's orbit around the Sun (you know these as the Summer Solstice, Fall Equinox, Winter Solstice, and Spring Equinox). There is a different form of astrology that uses the sidereal zodiac, and this method of prediction is based on the fixed constellations. Both methods (tropical versus sidereal) are valid but use differing techniques.

Roughly every 2,200 years we shift into a new astrological age that is represented by one of the 12 signs. We just completed what is known as the Age of Pisces, which is deeply connected to religion and Christ. The symbol of the fish has a long history and association with Christianity, and it should come as no surprise that the fish is the symbol of the sign Pisces, a mutable (meaning flexible) Water sign. In fact, the symbol of Pisces is two fishes swimming in opposite directions, which represents the pull and tension of duality that we all experience. The Age of Pisces woke us up to the fact that we are spiritual beings in the physical body. We are still working through the duality and fear that occurred when we lacked this information and knowing. In fact, we are still moving into the awareness that we (all of us) are made in the image and likeness of God and are of One community of consciousness.

The years as you know them reflect this entire process. Right now as I write this book, it is the year 2017. Anytime before the 0 year is termed BC (Before Christ), and that is roughly the beginning of the time frame of the Age of Pisces (lasting 2,166 years). Pisces is technically the last sign in the zodiac, but due to the backward movement of the Great Year, Pisces essentially resets the cycle. It's a good thing the years are reset to keep us aware of the great journey we are on together!

Due to the impact of each of the ages, the energy reaches beyond the 2,166-year divisions. That is why in the year 2017, we are entering the Age of Aquarius because we are essentially approaching the cusp. The whole process is felt like waves throughout humanity. There are no sharp turning points, but gentle waves that sweep us up and change our perspective. Some individuals in the collective will feel the energy early on as the wave initially begins to move (the spiritual forerunners). Eventually, everyone will feel the changes in their consciousness, but not at the exact same time, because, once again, it's a wave. I would assume (and these dates are highly debated by astrologers) that the technical start of the Age of Aquarius would be roughly around the year 2166. This is simply because I find it very significant that our calendar has been created with a 0 date in honor of Christ, and I find this to be of great importance.

In many ways, I wish that we called the astrological ages "waves" rather than "ages." Just like sound waves, the energy moves through us and changes the frequency of the collective consciousness. What is happening in the unseen eventually manifests in the physical world. In fact, we just experienced something quite remarkable to illustrate this spiritual evolution taking place on Earth. Recently, scientists discovered that the vibrational tone of the Earth has actually risen. Take a minute to let that sink in. There is a tone emitted from every planet, and the Earth's tone has literally changed to a higher vibration. I think that change is the beginning of the Wave of Aquarius. I hope you feel this in your bones and deep in your being.

Many of the New Agers and forerunners have been gravitating to the energy of Aquarius to usher it in to the collective since the 1970s. Once again, not everyone feels or experiences this. There will be some who don't feel this energy for another hundred years, and that is the nature of these transitions (no right or wrong with any of this). We don't all acclimate at the same time because we have that beautiful thing called free will, and that is very important. We also have our own individual karma and consciousness to work through, and that can at times hinder our ability in aligning with the broader energy. No matter what, just know that the wave will sweep through us all eventually.

The biggest impacts of the technological revolution have been the ability for people all around the world to stay connected and to empower themselves with knowledge. Not only that, but people are able to fly to different countries, experience different cultures, and learn about the world! I lived and worked in England, and it changed the way I viewed life as an American. It was the first time in my life that I saw a culture that didn't live to work, but worked to live.

My personal opinion is that technology will keep moving forward, and what feels like huge leaps to us now will eventually look like the little baby steps of the initial impact of the Age of Aquarius! Through the collective energy with the Age of Aquarius, there is a deep urge to give the power back to the people and to allow the individual to guide their own spiritual growth (specifically through inclusion, acceptance, and love). The energy of Aquarius can easily be felt through this powerful saying: "Give a man a fish and he'll eat for a day. Teach a man to fish and he will eat for his entire life." Aquarius wants everyone to eat for their entire life. Aquarius wants to teach and empower and is represented by the Water Bearer.

There is of course a great amount of resistant energy that must come up to be cleared with this movement. Those on the leading edge of the Aquarian energy are not necessarily the people currently in power. With our ability to question and change the tide, we are having to question the authority we have known. This was why in the 1980s there was an influx of new spirits called the Indigo Children. This is a movement I feel deeply connected to because I myself am an Indigo Child. We came hardwired to question authority, go our own way, and pave a new path. This wasn't easy, and the actions of the Indigo Children were easily misunderstood. Many of our behaviors were seen as acting out or being hard to control, and many times we came with a condition called ADD. ADD removes many of the filters because it neurologically prevents impulse control in an individual. There have been times in my life when I truly could not prevent certain things from coming out of my mouth. I personally believe that ADD and autism are spiritual conditions that support the growth of humanity over the long term (this doesn't mean that these conditions are easy, however, to integrate in the individual consciousness).

There was also an inner power to know when a person was lying, to see straight into another person's Soul, and to want to be as transparent as possible (regardless of consequences). These qualities took on a life of their own and were often unruly as the gifts were being honed. Indigo Children had a different set of internal criteria we lived by, and it wasn't always received with open arms. The Indigo Children were followed by the Crystal Children and then the Rainbow Children, but no child gave their parents the hell of a time that the Indigo Child did. Once again, the wave of energy sweeps through in perfect alignment with the full consciousness of humanity.

The astrological ages cover a wide span of time (2,166 years each). That's why when it comes to understanding the collective energy occurring year by year, I like to lean into another spiritual discipline called numerology. Numerology has the ability to add depth to certain techniques used in astrology and vice versa—astrology adds depth to numerology. My personal experience is that numerology allows us to see, feel, and understand the collective cycles that occur yearly in an easy format that is in alignment with the Age of Aquarius.

Numerology works with numbers and focuses very much on energy cycles (just like astrology, but using a different language). There are a total of nine cycles in numerology because of the significance of this single-digit number in mathematics. Once you go beyond the number 9, everything else can be broken back down into a root number or what is commonly known as a single digit. For instance, once you reach the number 10, you would break it down to a root number by adding the single digits together (1 + 0 = 1). This is why 10 really reflects a 1 cycle; because when you break down the number 10 to a single digit, it actually is resonating with a 1 in the energy cycle (although at a higher octave). Pretty cool stuff and super easy and fun to work with, which are my personal criteria for aligning with any and all spiritual techniques!

Any double digit can be broken down into a root number that reflects the energy cycle. However, in some cases, you will have to follow this simple method of reduction multiple times to reach the single digit. For instance, the number 989 would need to be broken down twice to finally reach its root energy.

First, you would add 9 + 8 + 9 and you would end up with the number 26.

At this point, you would further reduce the number to hit your single-digit root number by breaking down 26.

Now you are adding 2 + 6 and getting the number 8. Thus, 989 when it was completely broken down has the energy cycle of 8.

This is the basic mathematics behind discovering the energetic cycles present in numbers.

As I mentioned before, the collective energy is in us and influencing us. It is so deeply inside of us that we don't even recognize the significance. What we know is what we know, and we don't know what we don't. The collective energy is the backdrop to everything else that is unfolding in your life. If you imagine you are at the theater and you are watching a production of the *Lion King*, there are always two main things happening to create the experience. First, you have the actors who are singing, talking, and dancing, and secondly, you have the scenery and background. The collective energy is this background scenery, and it is important for us to be able to tap into and understand the influence of this energy.

Before you learn about the nine cycles, you will first complete the Vision Sheet instructions below to calculate the cycle movement that will be occurring throughout the year you are exploring. The cycles move numerically: the collective will move from a 1 year to a 2 year to a 3 year and so on. Once it hits a 9 year, it passes through what is called the zero zone during that actual year before moving into the next 1 year.

Remember (and this is important!): The collective energy shifts on January 1, when the year changes. This means that the collective cycles don't line up precisely with your year as viewed through astrology (birthdate to birthdate). For every year you explore through the book, the collective will be making their own shift from one cycle to the next. Once you get a hang of this simple numerology, it will be easy for you to see how the collective advances in a slightly different pattern.

Vision Sheet Instructions
Calculating the Collective Yearly Cycle

The first step is to calculate the collective yearly cycle number. As you may remember from chapter 1, the collective year is represented and explored through the traditional year that is celebrated on January 1. This marks the time when the number of the year changes, and through the number of the year, numerology offers its interpretation.

Because we are exploring your astrological year (from birthdate to birthdate), you will have already recorded at the top of your Vision Sheet the years you are currently exploring. For instance, if your birthdate is March 2 and you selected the year 2020, that means you are looking at the energy from March 2, 2020—March 2, 2021, and you would have written that information at the top of your Vision Sheet.

Step I:

Grab a piece of paper and pen to complete the simple mathematics by hand. You will be transferring the final information to your Vision Sheet at the end.

Part 1:

Write down the year that you are currently exploring. For instance, if you selected the year 2017 when you calculated your Cosmic Navigator, you would write that specific year down onto the piece of paper.

Part 2:

Now you will break down the year to its root number. To calculate the root number, you simply separate out the numbers of the year into single digits, then you will add those single digits together. Check out the example below:

Year: 2017

Breakdown to single digits: [2 + 0 + 1 + 7]

Add single digits together: [2 + 0+ 1+ 7 = 10]

Record final number = 10

* In this case, the final number is 10 and still is a double digit. This means we have to do the process again to reach the root number, which is a single digit.

Final number: 10

Breakdown to single digits: [1 + 0]

Add single digits together: [1 + 0 = 1]

Record final number = 1

The collective cycle number is 1.

Part 3:

Once you complete your calculations, record the collective cycle number onto the back of your Vision Sheet in the circle labeled "Collective Cycles."

STEP 2:

Although your cosmic calendar covers a one-year time span, it actually taps into two separate collective years. In our example, when you are looking at 2017, you are actually looking at 2017–2018. As your year unfolds, the collective cycles are switching on January 1 each year.

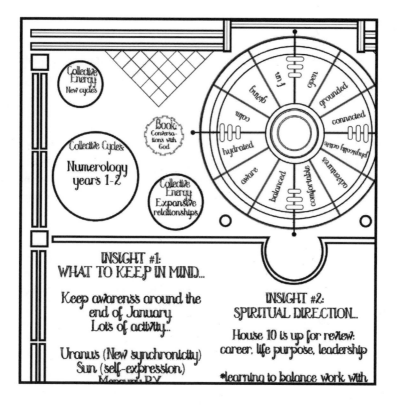

Part 1:

The collective always moves through the cycles numerically, so this means that you do not need to do the long mathematics again. You simply add 1 to the cycle you just calculated. For instance, if the collective was in a 1 year, it would next move into a 2 year. If it were in a 4 year, it would next move into a 5 year.

Note: If it is a 9 year, the collective moves next to a 1 year and restarts the cycle [The mathematics would be 9 + 1 = 10, with the further breakdown of 1 + 0 = 1]

Part 2:

Record the cycle that the collective will be moving into next by adding it into the circle labeled "Collective Energy." Using the example above, this would be read "Cycles: 1–2" in the circle,

Part 3:

It's time now to understand how the collective energy is influencing you and those around you. You will now read through the numerology meaning for both numbers activated on pages 14–15 Once you have completed that step, you will continue on.

Part 4:

Putting the pieces together is an important part of understanding the energy of your year. For this step, you will be writing two words or short phrases into the empty circles on the back side of the Vision Sheet (right next to where you wrote in the numerology numbers).

You know that I push for you to write out these insights. This time, it is so that you will have awareness of another person's perspective. Once again, you will see how this all fits together as your year unfolds. As you read the descriptions of the two numerology cycles, keep these questions in mind:

- What themes stood out to you?
- Were there any connections to what you have already explored in your year?
- Will these collective forces support you and align with your path? Or are they going in a different direction?

Part 5:

Once you have the two words or short phrases, please write them onto the Vision Sheet in the two larger circles surrounding the collective energy circle. You may reference the example Vision Sheet on pages 14–15 if needed.

Collective Cycles
Numerology Interpretation

1 Year:

The energy of a 1 year is harnessed in new beginning, new cycles, new energy, and NEW NEW NEW! This is about behaviors that break the current trends and set in motion new possibilities. The 1 year comes just after the 9 year and passes through what is called a zero zone (a space where outcome isn't easily predictable on any level). The 1 year often coincides with changes in the political system, leadership, and collective systems in general. You will feel it in your life as you start new projects or new jobs, meet new people, move/visit new locations, etc., etc.

2 Year:

The energy of a 2 year is all about relationships and elevating to the next level. This may seem like an easy year to understand, but it is highly dependent on the current relationships that are at play. This happens both at a collective level (think about the relationship between two countries) and a global level (think about the relationship between leaders), as well as on an individual level (think about the relationship with your boss, friends, family, et al.). Relationships are what support the Soul in evolving, and these years are about ensuring that you are in relationships that are expansive. The energy may up-level through what is experienced as breakthroughs, connections, commitments. Alternatively, the energy will move out and create space for a new experience: breakup, divorce, loss of employment, etc.

YEAR 3:

The energy of a 3 year is highly creative, fast, and optimistic. This is a year when you can feel the wind behind you as it supports you in moving forward. New inventions, ideas, and initiatives are all around, and there is a buzz within the collective and various groups. This is the glass half-full sort of year, and it lends itself well to new adventures, discoveries, and friendships. New ideas have the ability to create movement forward, and the bigger the leap, the more fear that can potentially surface. Often, many will avoid their idea or intuitive pull unconsciously because of fear. Depending on how you respond to the creativity within determines what occurs throughout this year. It can be either productive or explosive (or both) depending on the amount of fear being worked through.

YEAR 4:

The energy of a 4 year is about working toward a goal to bring it into manifestation. This is an emphasis on details, responsibility, structure, law, and rules. Although people tend to focus on the cons of structure, structure isn't inherently limiting. In fact, structure has the ability to create more choice, freedom, and empowerment. The 4 year will be addressing structure, and this often is seen in a working out or new agreement in the legal system. Collectively this can be seen through protests, laws being established, voting new people into office, and leadership adjustments. Individually, this can be seen through work, establishing new routines, difference of opinions in the workplace, etc.

YEAR 5:

The energy of a 5 year is all around change and the freedom of choice. This is the free-loving hippie energy that wants to be able to express whatever is the truth within. This is often seen collectively as a letting go and a having a "back to basics" attitude toward life. There is a level of simplification that gets exercised throughout the 5 year through choice—think about self-motivated career changes, new hobbies, spontaneous action taking. Collectively, you will see big political moves that speak for the minority, people leaving behind what they don't believe in, and an overall focus on freedom and a better life.

YEAR 6:

The energy of a 6 year is all about balance and learning to live from a space that honors work and play. In childhood, the emphasis is on play, and there is a fantasy of the freedom that comes when one is working as an adult. In adulthood, the emphasis is on work, and there is a fantasy of the freedom to play and do nothing in retirement. The year is about incorporating the energy of work and play into the now moment and not compromising (or waiting for a future moment to go back to the other extreme). In order to awaken to this conundrum, most will experience an extreme this year: boredom or overwhelmingness. Collectively, people are either overly stressed out and sick or extremely aloof and lost in thought. You'll start hearing people complain of boredom and lack of purpose, while those with too-many responsibilities will openly complain of stress and overwhelmingness. The answer is in the balance, not the extreme. This year works out the kinks to help all of us get there.

YEAR 7:

The energy of a 7 year is deeply spiritual and has an inward focus. There will be various awakenings that happen throughout this year on multiple levels, but all of equal importance. Focus within the individual is paramount, and anything that occurs is a reminder that peace out there will occur when peace inside is felt and experienced by everyone individually. The outer world is merely a mirror/reflection of the inner world, both individually and collectively. Don't forget that waking up is hard to do, and for those who aren't aware of the role they play, they may be shaken back into their awareness.

YEAR 8:

The energy of an 8 year is connected to inner power, authority, and stepping up and taking control. It's not unusual to experience intense power struggles throughout this year. This is because as people move into this power energy, they often start by learning to control the outside world, people, and experiences. This is why you will see many people who are new to the soapbox, those waking up to the soapbox, and those getting pushed off the soapbox. Why? Power is an internally fueled energetic of the Self. To feel Power because you have Power over other people isn't really inner power (because ultimately that "power" is dependent on something outside of the Self). The balance you see in the natural ecosystem of the Earth is reflective of the balance in all things, power included. Power is felt within and has nothing to do with the need to control. The way to learn this? Experience.

YEAR 9:

The energy of a 9 year is a culmination of all the cycles, and there are many endings throughout this time period. It's a finishing up of karma, unfinished business, and loose ends that were put to the side for later. Collectively, large corporations will close down, important officials will retire (or get fired), and older technology quickly is removed from the marketplace. It can be both a frustrating year and one of lightness and freedom, but it all depends on your perspective. You can actively work with this energy by decluttering your home, cleaning, and reorganizing, or by changing up your diet. As endings and closings sweep through, you can recognize and support others in seeing that a new chapter is now being written

VII

CHAPTER SEVEN

Your Spiritual
Direction

Each year as you experience your Solar Return, the planets will be in new positions, but even these movements over time reflect an even-bigger cycle and pattern. Although planetary circumstances will not return to the exact position they were in at the moment of your birth, there is a very obvious 33-year cycle that occurs through the Solar Return Chart. This is to say, if you were to remain in the same city as the one you were born in, many of the prominent planets and the Ascendant (the sign on the eastern horizon at the moment of your birth) and Midheaven (the sign at the southern highest point above the horizon) would be in a similar position to that of your natal/birth chart on your 33rd year. This pattern reveals an even-deeper unfolding of Spirit as it awakens. On your 33rd year, the overall impressions of the Solar Return Chart echo the desires of the Natal Chart, reflecting similar themes, dynamics, and patterns. This 33rd year marks a prime opportunity when you are reuniting with your spirit and entering a pivotal year of authentic awakening. In many ways, you truly begin to know your authentic Soul at this portion of your life journey as if you are waking up to yourself.

As the planets shift and rearrange to illuminate your life and purpose each year, there is one particular planet that is casting its light over that entire year. It is this force that is activating spiritual potential within you that SUPPORTS you in awakening. The planet that would be the next to rise into the sky after the Sun has made its Solar Return allows you to understand the underlying spiritual theme unfolding. I have personally found that by aligning with this information it will allow you to consciously operate from a space of peace and understanding. This is very important to me because I personally know that as you awaken spiritually, it can be difficult at times to find people to relate to or even talk to about what you are going through.

This section of the book and exploration of your Rising Planet is meant to get you acquainted with the area of your being that is being spiritually called to awaken. These are deep subjects, and there is no one way that the awakening process occurs. Your life is a chain of synchronicities supporting this process, but it is completely unique to you. By knowing the Rising Planet, you can explore the topic as much as you like. I have given book recommendations to support you further, but I encourage you to trust your inner voice and follow the path as you are inspired. We all are on such varying journeys that there is no one right way to awaken and expand. YOU are always your best guide, no matter what any spiritual guru tells you.

Vision Sheet Instructions
Your Spiritual Direction

Step I:

In table 1 of your Cosmic Navigator, one of the planets has been marked as *Rising. This signifies the Rising Planet of your chart.

Part 1:

Please write in the name of your Rising Planet on the back of the Vision Sheet in the blank circle just under the words "Cosmic Direction."

Part 2:

Take a moment to read about the significance of this planet on page 99. There is a cosmic direction associated with each planet. You can add this information below the name of your Rising Planet in the same circle.

Part 3:

Pulling from the text and the meaning of the Rising Planet, pick out one word or short phrase to enter into the blank circle just above where you entered your Rising Planet. This will serve to support you throughout your year.

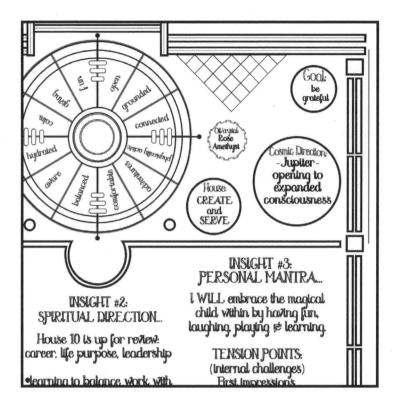

Goal:
be
grateful

Oil/crystal
Rose
Amethyst

Cosmic Direction:
- Jupiter -
opening to
expanded
consciousness

House:
CREATE
and
SERVE

INSIGHT #3:
PERSONAL MANTRA...

I WILL embrace the magical
child within by having fun,
laughing, playing & learning.

TENSION POINTS:
(internal challenges)
First impressions

INSIGHT #2:
SPIRITUAL DIRECTION...

House 10 is up for review:
career, life purpose, leadership

*learning to balance work with

STEP 2:

The Rising Planet in your chart connects back to a specific house in your yearly chart, and this is HOW you will be able to predict WHERE the energy around this transformation will manifest in your life.

Part 1:

Every planet in astrology is connected to a specific sign. This is what is being explored when you hear the term "rulership." You have just discovered the Rising Planet in your chart, and you will now determine what area of life this will impact. In order to do this, you have to connect a few more dots. I know astrology can feel complicated, but please just take your time and reach for the insight. You must now determine the astrological sign connected to your Rising Planet, and then we will take the next step. Use the chart below to see the sign associated with your Rising Planet.

Note: Some planets rule or are connected to more than one sign.

Rising Planet	Sign Connected
Sun	Leo
Moon	Cancer
Mercury	Gemini/Virgo
Venus	Taurus/Libra
Mars	Aries
Jupiter	Sagittarius
Saturn	Capricorn
Uranus	Aquarius
Neptune	Pisces
Pluto	Scorpio

Part 2:

Now that you know the sign or signs associated with your Rising Planet, we will connect one more dot. To see how the energy will be manifesting in your life, you must determine what house or houses the sign rules in the chart. Look to table 3 of your Cosmic Navigator to determine what house (or houses) the astrological sign rules. Write down the house or houses on your Vision Sheet in the blank circle to the left of where you entered your Cosmic Direction. Once you have recorded that information, you can look to the chart on page 110 to see HOW the energy will be showing up in your life. Once again, you will pick one word or a short phrase to add into the circle where you entered the house number affected.

STEP 3:

You are now sensing the spiritual direction that will be opening you up throughout the year. There have been book suggestions made when you were reading about your Rising Planet on page 99. If any of the books are familiar to you or have previously been recommended, or if you feel inspired by the name, I HIGHLY recommend reading the book. It's been my personal experience that when I receive a book recommendation from more than one source OR on more than one occasion, it is a sign that the energetics of the book will deeply support me on my path. You can record the book in the blank circle just to the right of "Collective Cycles." See reference Vision Sheet for guidance if needed on pages 14–15.

STEP 4:

Crystals and stones have long been used to support conscious awakening and growth. This is because naturally occurring formations like this carry within them a powerful vibration. They stay tuned to a specific frequency and will impact you accordingly. If you would like to strengthen your connection with the energetic forces of the Rising Planet in your chart, a recommendation is made based on the energetics of it on page 99. Record the recommended crystal into the blank circle to the left of the larger circle where you wrote in your Rising Planet and Cosmic Direction. If you feel inspired, I encourage you to purchase the crystal and keep it on your body or with you throughout the day.

Note: If the crystal bursts or breaks, it means you outgrew the vibration, and this is a normal phenomenon.

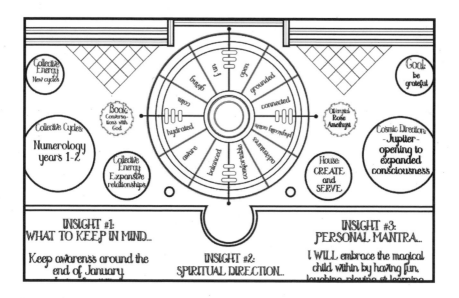

STEP 5:

One of the most powerful spiritual tools available to us is essential oils. Due to the nature of how they are created, we resonate with their properties and can carry them through all of our four bodies: physical body, etheric/vital body, emotional/astral body, and mental body. The recommended essential oil that is based on your Rising Planet will support you in moving the necessary energetics to open you up throughout your year. Be sure to find a reputable distributor that sells pure oils or you will not receive the same benefits. I recommend applying a single drop to the bottoms of your feet prior to meditation, when you are stressed out or when you feel out of alignment.

Record the essential oil on your Vision Sheet in the same blank circle as you did the crystal.

> Please note: You don't need to run out and purchase anything. I've included this because I've noticed there will be moments throughout the year when one desires something to support them or lift them up. These recommendations are given for those moments when you find that you need that new smell, new book, or new crystal.

COSMIC DIRECTION
Interpreting the Rising Planet

Cosmic Direction: The Sun
[Awakening the Ego]

With the Sun Rising, you are entering a year of extreme significance for your Soul development. As you evolve throughout your life, you come to many crossroads that force you to make powerful decisions that impact the overall course of your life. This could include deciding what university to attend, whether you would like to take that new job in a new city, whether you truly want to get married, or whether you will take a leap of faith and go after your dreams. Obviously, you are beginning to sense that this year will be highly significant for you. As you approach these decisions, it is imperative that you begin to cultivate a deeper relationship with your High Self so that you can take the best course of action (the one that leads you to the Soul growth you wanted for this life). One way that you can gauge if you are making the correct Soul decision is to ensure that it aligns with your Soul and NOT just your Ego. The Ego tends to be motivated by outward accumulation, money, fame, and fortune (especially when it is fully identified with the physical world). The Soul tends to be motivated by love, passion, growth, and service. While there are certainly no wrong choices because we live in an expanding Universe, there are what I call "slow" choices. Slow choices still achieve growth, but, as you might guess . . . slowly. Trust your gut, listen to your inner voice, and make the decisions that feel right in your bones. This year is about listening to YOU, taking actions that align for YOU, and not relying on other people to tell you who you are.

Recommended reading: *7 Spiritual Laws* by Deepak Chopra
Recommended essential oil: Lemon and wild orange oil
Recommended crystal: Citrine
Numerology: The Sun vibrates as the number 1

Cosmic Direction: The Moon
[Awakening the Astral/Emotional Body]

With the Moon Rising you are approaching a very emotional year that is allowing you to connect with others on an even-deeper level. The Moon rules your instinctual self (the you that reacts before thinking and often gets you into trouble). It is deeply connected to what is called your Astral/Emotional Body and is influenced through what are known as the twin forces: the Law of Attraction and the Law of Repulsion. These forces are the underlying current that magnetizes you into certain people, places, and events OR repels you from certain people, places, and events.

As your year unfolds, you may feel overly emotional at times or as if you are constantly being swept up into yourself and then released (just like the tide). Rather than panicking over this newfound emotional intensity, I would like to encourage you to lean into it and LEARN how to interpret it in your life. No emotion is inherently good or bad, but acting on an emotion without awareness can lead to further difficulties. For instance, the magnetic pull we feel to people or places isn't always of a positive nature. It's important to begin to see connections that you may have previously discounted. Pay attention to when you feel magnetized to something, versus repelled, and document in a journal the before/during/after effect of following those feelings (this supports you in developing spiritual discernment). You can learn a lot about yourself and others throughout this year if you consciously attune to what is happening to you.

Recommended reading: *The Untethered Soul* by Michael Singer
Recommended essential oil: Ylang ylang, rose
Recommended crystal: Moonstone
Numerology: The Moon vibrates to the number 2

Cosmic Direction: Mercury
[Awakening the Inner Speaker]

With Mercury Rising you will have a year that is focused on connection, communicating, and thinking. Depending on your circumstances, you will be called forward to continue to hone each of these skills. When it comes to connecting, this is about developing empathy and compassion. You will be learning and developing the ability to see from another person's point of view. This ultimately leads you to a space where you begin to see that not everything that occurs in this world can fall into a right or wrong category. This of course is a pivotal step in transcending dualistic thinking, and you can begin to see the intricate connections between connection, communicating, and thinking.

How we think impacts how we communicate. Who you are inside will at some point match who you are on the outside in full TRUTH. This means that you will no longer alter your true emotions or opinions to meet society's standards of right/wrong. This thinking you is the most underdeveloped spiritual asset because it believes it exists in complete separation (it is driven by fear and takes actions to remain safe). Throughout this year, you will begin to expand in whatever area is most appropriate for your growth.

Recommended reading: *Change Your Thoughts, Change Your Life* by Wayne Dyer

Recommended essential oil: Peppermint

Recommended crystal: Clear quartz, black tourmaline

Numerology: Mercury vibrates to the number 5

Cosmic Direction: Venus
[Opening the High Heart]

When Venus is rising in the yearly chart, you are embarking on a very exciting year. Venus rules many things near and dear to our heart, most importantly love and relationships. In addition to this, Venus rules our values, money, and assets. This is a year of expansion for you, and you will be opening up your heart to deeper levels of love. Love comes in many forms: self-love, life partnership, family, friendship, mentors, etc. It is about Soul and heart connecting that advances you into a new space in your life.

You will begin to soften over the year, lose some inner judgment of yourself and others, and step into a space of compassion and connection. Venus is about celebrating the pleasures of the physical plane, but not being led by them. Keep this all in mind as the year unfolds and you begin to connect with new and different people. What is the deeper Soul connection that is taking place? What part of your being is being expanded through these relationships? How can you consciously choose to open yourself up?

Recommended reading: *What's in the Way Is the Way* by Mary O'Malley
Recommended essential oil: Lavender, rose
Recommended crystal: Rose quartz
Numerology: Venus vibrates to the number 6

Cosmic Direction: Mars
[OPENING TO INSPIRED ACTION]

The year that Mars is rising in your chart is a year of action, integrating masculine energies and tapping into the formula for ultimate success on your path (and no, I'm not just talking about money). All the right intentions within you will lead to zero growth if you do not align them with inspired action. Mars rules action and supports the process of taking thought form and making it manifest. There will be a burning desire within you to take more action and to move along your path. For the spiritual seeker, this often is about sharing what you have learned and experienced. There is only so much knowledge one is allowed to take in without using it in service to the whole.

These actions forward take courage and determination because Mars acts as a trigger for NEW behaviors that support NEW outcomes. As you begin to connect with this energy, it's important not to let it take you over. You can take so much action that it renders you ineffective in your pursuits. Taking action in too-many directions will backfire and water down the power behind all of your actions. Feel the passion in your heart and then focus on discerning where the action and the impulse is coming from. The energy of Mars will tend to focus on the areas of your life that have become stagnant and need to begin circulating again. It can be uncomfortable to step outside your comfort zone, but when you have the energy of Mars supporting you, you find the courage to do it anyway.

Recommended reading: *Feel the Fear and Do It Anyway* by Susan Jeffers
Recommended essential oil: Cinnamon, clove
Recommended crystal: Jasper (grounds you)
Numerology: Mars vibrates to the number 9

Cosmic Direction: Jupiter
[OPENING TO YOUR EXPANDED CONSCIOUSNESS]

With Jupiter Rising in your chart, you are in for a spiritually expansive year. It's important to remember why we all are here on Earth, and it is the same reason for all of us. We are learning to connect and awaken to who we really are. This is not an easy process, and it is very painful as we release and expand over and over again.

Jupiter is a planet that brings gifts and supports us in a positive and uplifting way (just don't let it go to your head and take it for granted!). You will most likely be provided an opportunity throughout this year to step deeper into your power in a specific area of your life. Take the time to appreciate the journey and to know that you are supported on your path. There are points in your life when you will fear that you have been forgotten or that the Universe no longer is supporting you. I can guarantee that this universal power that is in all of us never ceases; it is always working within the energetic lines that lead to our expansion as a whole and as an individual. The power that brings you miracles and synchronicities is the same power that takes them away. You are being guided every moment of your day, even when you can't perceive it.

Recommended reading: *Conversations with God* by Neale Donald Walsh
Recommended essential oil: Rose
Recommended crystal: Amethyst
Numerology: Jupiter vibrates to the number 3

Cosmic Direction: Saturn
[Transcending Separation Consciousness]

With Saturn Rising, you are headed into a year that will push you outside your comfort zone. The older we get, the harder and harder it is for us to move out of our comfort zone and push eagerly (without fear) for growth. This is because as the years go on, we form beliefs and more filters by which we view the world. This does of course serve you for a time, but what happens throughout your path is that you will discover that your truth changes and so does your perspective. Your operating system will in fact need to be upgraded, and sometimes a full reboot is necessary.

One of the most important transitions you will experience is the shifting from a duality lens (separation) into a heart-centered lens (connection). Saturn is a tough teacher and it honestly won't take no for an answer. You will have an opportunity to push through to the next level, and if you can release judgment and grow, Saturn will help you do this through your experiences.

We live in a Saturn-ruled Universe, but we are breaking through its barriers and cultivating our own sense of authority (and believe it or not, Saturn works to teach you to be your own authority). This means that you will be working on cultivating your own personal power and have the opportunity to express it. Do this meaningfully and with purpose as your year unfolds.

Recommended reading: *The Master Game* by Robert Ropp
Recommended essential oil: Sandalwood
Recommended crystal: Choose whatever speaks to you (this is you practicing your own authority)
Numerology: Saturn vibrates to the number 8

Cosmic Direction: Uranus
[SELF ACCEPTANCE]

With Uranus Rising in your chart, you have a very interesting and most likely different type of year coming up for you. Uranus is ruler of the unusual, strange, and different. The important thing to remember with all of this is that what we view as unusual, strange, and different is simply due to a lens we have inherited in viewing our world. This is often reflective of our family values, community values, and the inherent perspective of our country of origin. In fact, what one would find strange in the Western world is perfectly normal in the Eastern world (take astrology, for example).

The root of moving out of norm is very much a strategic art in stretching our consciousness so that we are able to create self-acceptance. This is not only for ourselves, but for us all. The range of HOW you will experience this is all over the place (thank Uranus for that one!). It typically involves random happenings, unexpected encounters, and accidents that aren't really "accidents." Stay open to the possibilities of the year and you will be impressed with the cleverness of the planet Uranus.

Recommended reading: *Return to Love* by Marianne Williamson
Recommended essential oil: Frankincense
Recommended crystal: Rose quartz, quartz (acceptance and amplification)
Numerology: Uranus vibrates to the number 4

Cosmic Direction: Neptune
[SPIRITUAL DISCERNMENT]

With Neptune Rising in your chart, you will go through a transformation this year that allows you to see more clearly. I often say that this is the type of year when you are removing the rose-colored glasses and seeing things as they truly are. Neptune is an all-loving, empathetic source, but it is also representative of the blind spot where we don't see clearly. In many ways, Neptune is wanting us to perceive the ultimate eternal truth that we all come from the exact same source. BUT here is the important thing to consider: multiple (and contradictory) truths can exist on multiple levels at the EXACT same time. Meaning that you can know that someone's Spirit is beautiful, kind, and loving, but you can simultaneously know that the person is moving through a separated expression that isn't.

This problem is one of discernment, and many people bounce to extremes. Being "all loving" and ignoring the negative has led many New Agers to be taken advantage of, getting lost and losing their sense of self. Take time to see the truths that exist on multiple levels throughout this year. This will empower you to live your life in your own truth and authenticity during this year of practicing nonjudgment and holding strong boundaries.

Note: With Neptune Rising, you would do well to seek second opinions, not make assumptions, and keep an eye on the motivations and experiences you have with others. Often, you see your hidden enemy, and it isn't always who you thought it was.

Recommended reading: *The 4 Agreements* by Don Miguel Ruiz
Recommended essential oil: Peppermint
Recommended crystal: Obsidian
Numerology: Vibrates to the number 7

Cosmic Direction: Pluto
[Spiritual Rebirth]

With Pluto Rising, you are in for a big ride that culminates in deep self-transformation. Most of the time, these transformations are the ones you put off, avoided, and tried not to get involved with. You know, the skeletons in the closet. It's important to remember that whatever you hide inside, you are actually holding on to and storing. You can do this for only so long before something will trigger you in the outer world to work through the emotions and release them from the physical body. This is because the physical body isn't meant to be a storage unit.

Take a moment to remember and reflect on a beautiful memory you have had: perhaps the birth of a child, sitting in front of the ocean on vacation, or simply going for a massage. Now, take a second to recognize how you feel and the space where that memory comes from. It almost feels like it moves through you, right? Or that you are able to pull it from an invisible library that feels light and free.

Take another moment to call up a bad memory, one that makes you cringe. Can you feel how it comes from within the body? It is hard to feel and you somehow "push it down" or "away"? This is because negative emotions that aren't felt, processed, and released get stored in the physical body.

Pluto Rising is wanting to make sure you have enough storage space available in your physical body to function, be healthy, and be happy. Think of your body as a portable flash drive that can carry only so much data. Pluto helps you sort this out and is always working on your behalf (even when you can't see it). The best thing to do is to let go, surrender, and accept that what comes to you is actually helping you in ways you never could imagine.

Recommended reading: *I Am the Word* by Paul Selig

Recommended essential oil: Jasmine

Recommended crystal: Moldavite

Numerology: Vibrates to any number (it goes where the tune is off)

COSMIC DIRECTION
WHERE YOU WILL BE
EXPERIENCING GROWTH BY HOUSE

HOUSE 1: SELF

YOU will be impacted the most with this energy, and it is deeply connected to how you perceive yourself. This house more than any other is about the SELF and learning how to live the life you want. The most important piece is that when one reflects on the Self, there can be confusion, because what Self are you living from? The Infinite or High Self that incarnates multiple times? Or the you that is here now and has a set of wants and desires? The energy will be moving you forward on this deeper journey of awakening, and you will most certainly have an opportunity to make decisions that are connected with your Self and what YOU want.

HOUSE 2: FINANCES/WORK

Your finances and values are always what tends to come up for an individual when this house gets activated. There will be a pull to reassess and ensure that you are financially secure, and this will be of huge importance to you throughout the year. You may find yourself dealing with some sort of money issue (both good or bad) throughout the year. You need to find a way to balance between wanting security for your happiness versus greed for your Ego. Often there will be new ventures or new opportunities through business or career that arrive during this time.

HOUSE 3: SIBLINGS, CLOSE FRIENDS

The third house really reflects on the people who are with you most consistently throughout your life. This could be your siblings or your best friend whom you have known since you were five years old. These relationships are unique in that they begin to see you from the most expanded perspective. For example, that year you shaved your head and got a tattoo? It's perceived very differently by the friend you've known since you were five versus the friend who was getting the tattoo with you. These are the relationships that anchor us to ourselves when we go through our ups and downs. There will be a reconnection in some manner to these important relationships in your life throughout the year. If you have been unable to prioritize these relationships in your life, I encourage you to make the effort to set up a time to really connect back in with them. These are the people who seem to reflect us in the truest way and with the most power. When we are lost, they always seem to be found (and vice versa).

HOUSE 4: FAMILY

The energy will be moving through your identification with your family. This is a shifting process throughout your life because for the first large portion, you were the child with the parents, the siblings, or both. That was your nuclear family, and your world revolved around them: They were your center planets, if you will. Then as you grow, you create your own new planetary system, and the energy begins to shift. Your originally nuclear family is now YOUR family, and you begin to take action and gravitate around the needs of this new unit. The energy moves here and supports the natural progression and orbit of these pivotal people in your life. Everything that is outside the "nuclear family" is a "far outer planet" in your solar system of *being*. It is very important to honor and create flowing cycles to support you on your path. This year you will become aware of this. Ask yourself: Who is in your Universe? Who is rotating in orbit harmoniously? Who is not?

HOUSE 5: CREATION

There is to be some sort of creation and something new brought into your life. Whether this is a pet, child, loved one, business idea, or book is something that you will need to decide. You are primed and ready to create and add something new into your life that is through your heart center and from your Soul. I find this is an exciting year for artists because their passion is flowing and the muse will strike at any moment. You will need to tap into this creative force and use it for the highest good of all. If you get stopped by fear, shift straight into the need for service. I was very scared to share my writing with the world. It was the mere thought of my writing having the potential to help even one person that got me through. This was my personal thought that saw me through some massive fear: Could I stomach the process of me moving through fear to allow even just one person to move into more light? The answer was of course YES. The irony is that I myself moved into more light through that process.

HOUSE 6: DAILY HABITS

How you go about your day is how you go about your life. When you want real change you start at the nucleus of change: your day. You will be changing something about your daily habits, and this could be a change in work, eating habits, or exercise routine, or even the addition of a pet. When the energy shows up in this house you will be making the micro change that leads to the macro change in your life. This often takes more willpower than many of the other houses because these changes stem from you. Even if you get a serious illness and the doctor tells you to change what you eat and start exercising, the change still ultimately must come through you. There is often some hushed whisper we hear telling us to change. It is a shame that we often wait for the catalyst of suffering to listen. This is the year to commit and act.

HOUSE 7: RELATIONSHIPS

While this house rules all types of relationships, it tends to emphasize romantic relationships and marriage. The energy here will be expressing through the partnership that you have invested the most amount of time into. This is that which is most near and dear to your heart. Relationships that are healthy tend to get a makeover. Relationships that are unhealthy also get a makeover (it's just a different type). All underlying dynamics will tend to surface through the year. Much of what you previously ignored or avoided will begin to come up as well. Please keep in mind that this is a good thing. This means more communication, experiences taken together, and growth together.

If you are single and you don't have that relationship near and dear to your heart, you may just find that you are connecting with someone this year. You may experience the old saying, "when it rains it pours." Don't shy away from being yourself, and stay in your truth. The best partnerships are those that support us in expressing our most positive aspects (and help us outgrow that which was limiting).

HOUSE 8: SELF-TRANSFORMATION

There are beautiful moments when self-transformation occurs and a new you is literally born. These are the pivotal turning points of our lives that shape us and help us become who we truly want to be. The transformation of the physical body is seen through losing weight and getting in shape. The transformation associated with this house is NOT about the physical, but about the inner you (the one who is deciding who you are and the choices you make). It's a pity that the physical body does not adequately reflect the amount of changes that take place within the individual.

You have been reborn within hundreds if not thousands of times. Each time, you are more expanded, centered, and balanced. The hardest part here is if you need or seek external proof to validate the inner transformation you've gone through. If the "external proof" or "validation" isn't there, you may accidentally doubt yourself and fall backward, going spiritually retrograde. It takes time for the inner transformation to fully come through, and there will be a lag in the physical world. Think of it this way: They are watching last season's version of you and haven't caught up yet. No big deal. They are going to be super surprised with this plot twist they didn't see coming!

HOUSE 9: LEARNING/EDUCATION

The energy is flowing through your mind, and you will be expanding what you know. You may be reading, writing, studying, and going to workshops many times throughout this year. It is about creating a foundation of knowledge that provides you an opportunity to learn/apply new skills. Keep in mind, this doesn't just reflect the traditional schooling model of learning. There is the school of hard knocks out there in the real world. Lessons and knowledge that you need on your Soul's path will be coming through in spades this year. Whether this is something you teach to yourself or something you apprentice in with another, the quest is the same: accumulate wisdom. Where can you actively learn more and expand?

HOUSE 10: YOUR CALLING (CAREER)

For many people their calling comes through their career, but this is not a hard and fast rule. If your calling is to be a mother, that is still your calling whether you keep working at a job for someone else or take that job at home. Discovering and being comfortable with our calling is a whole other game. This is because we are taught what we should be/do/have. There is a clear program: Go to school, get good grades, graduate, and get a job working for someone else. If your calling falls outside this, you have to break the habits that hold you back. You must follow your heart because it would never lead you in the wrong direction. As much as we want to be told what our calling is, that would ultimately defeat the point, wouldn't it? This is something that comes forth from within you, and it has always been with you. Think back on your life and what you have dreamed about since you were a child. What have you always loved doing? What can you do in the physical world that literally stops time? It is my suspicion that the actions we take where time melts away are always pointing us to our gift.

HOUSE 11: FRIENDSHIPS / YOUR CHOSEN PEOPLE

Throughout your life you will have various friendships that come and go. There is a direct correlation between your personal growth and the friendships that surround you. This is because energy is contagious, and you pick up on the habits and mannerisms of those you spend time with.

You will most likely have your inner circle shift or expand throughout the year. This may be because you've taken a new direction: think about work, geographical location, political, spiritual, etc. When these transitions occur, your friendships transition as well. This can be painful depending on the circumstances but is ultimately allowing you to move forward. Think about what you believe friendship to be: Whom do you look for in a friend? What do you seek?

HOUSE 12: SPIRITUALITY/RELIGION

This year is an awesome one that gets to the heart of all things . . . transcending and finding peace and harmony within. All of us have a different set of beliefs, and it is vital to remember that there is no one path to Heaven/Nirvana/God. The main idea is that at some point you arrive and we all do! It doesn't matter the path we took.

This year is about connecting in with people or places that are kindred to your beliefs and your path. When you surround yourself with people traveling on a similar trajectory in consciousness expansion, you will find much of the support you need for the journey. The coming together to share beliefs is a beautiful thing, but also often leads to some very common missteps on the path. Stay aware of your beliefs, intentions, and actions through all spiritual growth. The most important thing to keep in mind is that there is no one way: stay open, appreciate diversity, and respect those around you.

CHAPTER EIGHT

Making the Most of Your Year

Astrology is a tool, not a life manager. It is not meant to micromanage your actions, take away your free will, or lead you to believe that all of life is fated and can be predicted (because it's not). Astrology works best when you approach it with a broad lens, seek the patterns, and align with the cosmic forces through this deeper awareness. The energetic impacts of working with astrology is beyond anything you could receive from another outlet, because it tunes into the always fluctuating Universal Grand Design.

When I first started doing yearly astrological readings, I was obsessed with them. During this phase of my business, I was creating handmade scrolls that depicted the yearly chart, and made predictions for three specific and important months for the individual. When clients saw the 12 months of their year broken up and were able to review the energetics, there was this deep sense of empowerment that filled them. They had gained the aerial view and they had curiosity around the understanding of their year.

What I discovered, however, was that no matter how powerful the initial exploration of their year, the true magic unfolded as the year progressed and they EXPERIENCED everything that was seen.

You will be able to see these patterns and understand them **now**, but they support you most when you are energetically experiencing them **later**. For instance, if you have a huge event happen in your life that completely triggers you AND you then are able to look at your Vision Sheet, it's profound. You will be reminded of something in that moment that supports you in changing your perception and shifting your experience to a higher expression.

This is why I had you create a Vision Sheet, so that you can come back to it when you feel called to throughout your year. Chances are, you will turn to it when you are feeling off or unsettled, and I fully support this. We need the tool of astrology to ground us, expand our perspective, and support us in moving forward consciously on our path. I cannot say this enough: What you are doing **now** will support you **later**. There will be a moment in your year when you will connect with your Vision Sheet, and all this will make sense—you will truly see what you believe you are hearing now.

All of us experience spiritual checkpoints in our lives, and these are powerful catalysts for our expanding consciousness. These are often experienced as deja vu or fate, and you have a strange sense and awareness of having been in that experience before. These moments are important because they are supporting us on multiple levels. When we experience these checkpoints, we are hitting a sort of growth spurt on our paths.

Another form of spiritual checkpoint is seeing your astrological chart because it activates potential within you. I believe a person sees their chart only when they are ready to see their chart. Crazy enough, when I was in elementary school I went to visit my friend's aunt who lived in California. Her aunt was actually an astrologer, and though I could have magnetized into this area of study at that point, I didn't. I remember she printed things out for me and wanted to talk to me about my chart, and I couldn't hold focus at all. I didn't even see my chart. I know now that I wasn't capable of interpreting it at that point in my life. When you visually see and experience the knowledge within your chart, you have arrived at a powerful point on your path. There is growth activating on all levels of your being: physical body, astral/emotional body, mental body, and spiritual body.

I share this all to remind each of us that we are completely supported. You haven't missed your opportunity or messed anything up; that's impossible. I look back and reflect on that synchronicity of meeting an astrologer and staying with one when I was a teenager, and yet nothing opened or happened within me. I realize now it's okay that I didn't magnetize into this art at that point, because I wasn't ready. The cool thing? The Universe kept offering me opportunities until I was ready.

I want to share with you how it came back around in hopes that my story of missed opportunity, low self-esteem, fear, and a very intense inner speaker didn't actually mean I was broken. It meant I was in the process of becoming whole again.

Of course, I'm leaving out all the sad, dark stuff because that will probably be another book. I missed lots of opportunities, got fired from jobs, couldn't listen to anybody, and very rarely could get control of myself. Astrology was something special for me, and it wasn't astrology per se, but merely the belief in the something more. It tipped the scale. Here is how astrology did come back around.

Just after my husband and I moved into an apartment together, I started to get an intuitive pull to move. It made no sense: our lease wasn't up, we didn't have the money, and my whole family told me no. In fact, I got two calls from my father and brother telling me I was nuts. However, I knew on all levels of my being that we were supposed to buy a house. I don't know how, but I just knew.

I have had these pulls at different moments of my life, and I learned to just move with them rather than fight against them. To buy a house was what we needed to do, and I wouldn't bend on this. I was relentless and stubborn. We searched and searched until we found a house that I knew was the house we were meant to live in. Meanwhile, my husband didn't really like it, and my dad still tried to talk me out of it! BUT, that is the thing with me, when I know, I KNOW. And I knew. I just didn't know why. We never really do know the why in the moment.

We bought the house, and when we moved into it, we discovered that the previous owner had left all sorts of things behind. There were old records in the garage, paint cans in the basement, and some very random things. After moving in, we discovered a set of dusty old encyclopedia books and one very special book in the back closet of our third small bedroom. It was that book that changed the course of my entire life. I picked that book up, and it smelled like an old antique bookstore on the streets of London.

I loved that magical book and discovering it in our house, but when I tried to read it, I couldn't comprehend it. Once again, I wasn't ready.

Years later, I was.

That book explained astrology in a unique way that supported me in taking my first steps.

It was in fact years later when I was on maternity leave that I actually sat down and began to read it. Ironically, I did it only because I became angry, and that anger motivated me enough to commit to one thing and not give up. I needed to break a pattern, and there was that book, sitting there waiting for me on my bookshelf. In that moment, I chose to learn astrology no matter the cost. No matter how many years it would take me. No matter if I was no good and it led nowhere. You see, the Universe never stopped giving me chances. It's the same for everyone. These powerful opportunities to connect with our gifts are there, and they are not forgetting us—we are forgetting them.

Strangely, that commitment was what led me somewhere beyond astrology. It was the commitment that was the true catalyst.

Astrology reignited my passion of writing, and I never could have logically seen how they came together. My writing was my joy, but I didn't think people would like it because often they didn't. This was something that I struggled with and had to work through. I'm terrible at spelling and grammar. I make words up. I was always told to keep writing poetry, and that my fiction was poor (multiple professors, multiple students). I didn't get great feedback in workshops, and I was so nervous I could barely speak. I was constantly needing to participate for grades, and I would freak out because I didn't want to sound stupid. I still wrote because I loved it, but I didn't think I had any real gift that would be of service to anyone but myself.

I did get into a master's program for writing, but once again, they said to write poetry and not fiction. And honestly, even though I got into the program, I kind of felt like a fraud. I knew I was there for a reason, but it wasn't in my mind because I was a great writer. I felt like somehow I must have accidentally tricked the system or something to get in (I knew it was in many ways fated, which made me doubt my talent even more). I was always afraid of what people would say, but I knew I had to keep trying. Somewhere, somehow, the small, still voice that told me to keep trying became something I learned to listen to and trust.

I don't know your journey, but I know enough now to realize we all are moving through the same fear. We all have these pieces inside us that we hide. This process of hiding stunts our growth and causes us to live in isolation and alone (stuck in there). Wherever you are, I hope this book can support you in sharing your truth. We have a shared history of moving through this, and I want you to know, as crazy as it sounds, I believe in you.

Your yearly chart is a form of support and guidance. It is the warm hug of the divine offering you insight into how your path is unfolding so that you can make the highest-possible choices. Please know that this gift of astrology is straight from the all-being consciousness of the One, the Universe. It reflects your Soul pattern and speaks directly to you. All I have done is provide you a method for piecing this information together, but the message is ultimately yours.

To bring this all home, you will be completing your yearly chart and creating your visual representation for your year. This is where you will feel the magic begin to infuse your Vision Sheet as you create that checkpoint and move with the energy.

Vision Sheet Instructions
Completing Your Yearly Chart

Step I:

The large circle in the middle of the front page of your Vision Sheet is representative of a typical astrological chart. It has 12 segments that reflect the 12 astrological houses and, in the yearly chart, correlate with the energy of the 12 months of your year. The house numbers are already notated for you and have been written in with numerical numbers 1–12 on your Vision Sheet.

Part 1:

The signs of the zodiac are pulled into the 12 houses and create the energy dynamics and expressions for your year. This is based on the moment the Sun returns to its natal starting point (i.e., one more slinky ring out). In table 3 of your Cosmic Navigator, you will be able to see the signs that rule each of the houses in your yearly chart.

A: Determine the sign ruling house 1 in table 3 of your Cosmic Navigator.

B: Look to the chart below to identify the glyph that represents that sign.

C: Write the glyph into the raindrop shape located closest to the house number. See
    example Vision Sheet for guidance.

D: Continue this process for the remaining 11 houses.

SIGN	GLYPH
ARIES	♈
TAURUS	♉
GEMINI	♊
CANCER	♋
LEO	♌
VIRGO	♍
LIBRA	♎
SCORPIO	♏
SAGITTARIUS	♐
CAPRICORN	♑
AQUARIUS	♒
PISCES	♓

Step 2:

In chapter 2, you created your cosmic calendar and determined the dates of your year that are associated with the astrological houses. You have already written those dates into the 12 outer squares that surround your yearly chart. You will be moving these dates directly into your yearly chart as another way of perceiving and viewing the energy of your year.

Part 1:

Look to the outer squares on the left-hand side of the yearly chart. Just below the Roman numeral "I" you entered a set of dates (this is your birthdate plus 30 days). Once you have located this time frame, you will be transferring it into your yearly chart.

Part 2:

Look at the time frame below the Roman numeral I and see if the date falls toward the beginning or ending of the month. Depending on how the dates fall, you will choose what month to write into the blank outer segment of the circle in the center of the Vision Sheet. For example, if the date is May 25–June 25, you would round it and just write June into the first segment (the space just below the number 1 in the yearly chart). You can reference the example Vision Sheet for reference on pages 14–15. If the date falls on the 15th of the month, I recommend defaulting to the earlier month, for example, for March 15, you would write in March.

Part 3:

Continue this process until you have transferred all of the months.

STEP 3:

You will now enter the planets into the appropriate astrological houses to complete your chart. In table 1, columns 1 and 4, you will be able to identify the annual house location for each of your planets either by writing the name of the planet or drawing in the glyph.

Part 1:

Locate the Sun in table 1, column 1, and its annual house location in column 4. Enter the word "Sun" or draw in the glyph, using the chart below, into the appropriate house of your yearly chart.

Part 2:

Continue this process for the Moon, Mercury, Venus, Mars, Jupiter, Saturn, Uranus, and Pluto.

Part 3:

Make sure to transfer the "yearly gift" and "yearly lesson" to the corresponding segment in the middle chart.

STEP 4:

Take a moment to connect with the visual impact of your yearly chart.

Part 1:

What stands out to you in your yearly chart? What is the time frame associated with that part of your chart?

Part 2:

Take a few minutes to connect and write down anything that comes to you in the Insights section. I've said it before and I'll say it again: What you are doing now will support you later.

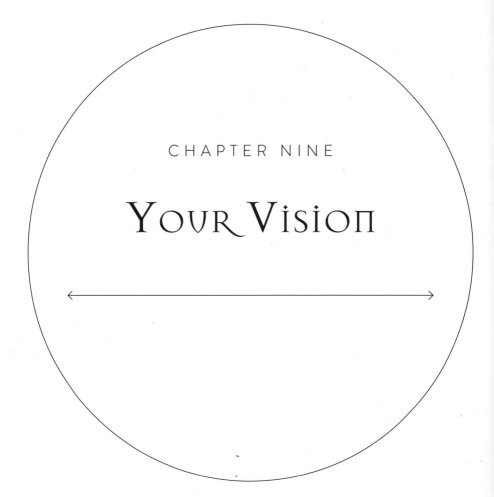

CHAPTER NINE

Your Vision

There is no true ending to this book, because it is an energetic spiral. When you've completed YOUR year and moved through one Vision Sheet, you will find yourself back at your next slinky ring. When you approach your birthdate again, this book will be here for you, but it will have changed, and so will you and your Vision Sheet. This book and your journey will never be identical again because it is expanding and YOU are expanding. This means that things you read before may feel like they have disappeared, and you will read things for the very first time (the second time).

You have now decoded your yearly chart and have recorded everything you need to take with you for your year. This is your cosmic compass, and it will be ready for you whenever you need it. What you are doing **now** will support you **later**.

People often align with the January 1 date to create their vision for their year because of the emphasis on New Year's resolutions. This is in fact a great time to set intentions for collective groups, but I do not personally believe that this is the most powerful time to set intentions for the individual. This could help explain why even with the greatest intentions, New Year's resolutions often fail. When it comes to the individual, the birthdate is the most important time, in my opinion, for creating these types of goals and vision. Of course, this has all to do with the slinky ring and the energetic step you take into YOUR new cycle at the time of your Solar Return (birthdate).

When you live each year of your life to its full potential, you will inevitably live your entire LIFE to its full potential. This book is truly a cosmic compass, and it grew from my desire to support others in an empowering way. Year by year, you will continue on your path, and with the support of this ancient practice of astrology, you do so in alignment with the cosmos. You will be infused with powerful intentions, deeper awareness, and a passion in your heart.

We are in the fuzzy, inspiring part of this beautiful process right now. These insights are real, but they still need to be applied.

Knowledge is just knowledge until it is thoughtfully applied and mastered, transforming then into wisdom.

To guide yourself, you must consciously be aware of the energy you want to experience. This is about learning to focus on what you do want in life, and when you do, your perspective and experience do shift. The mind is a brilliant friend that can search and amplify your environment. As it does this, you begin to see new opportunities, and doors magically appear. Of course this isn't magic, it's about shifting perspective. Those things were ALWAYS there; your mind was just focused in a different direction. In a world that has us looking for what is wrong, we easily get stuck in these emotional downward spirals. They aren't healthy, and it is truly a shame that this happens and isn't explored both from a spiritual and scientific perspective.

When I was a manager, I discovered how disastrous it was to look for the imperfection or weakness and focus on it. When I was first trained, I was developed to ultimately look for what was wrong and then fix it. This was the same approach taken with goal setting and generating sales growth. None of these methods or approaches felt right to me, because the underlying focus didn't ultimately serve my true intentions.

One day, I was doing a walking meditation, and I had a vision. I saw my entire team as a symphony orchestra of instruments playing beautiful music together. It hit me in that moment: The trumpet is perfect the way it is; the flute is perfect the way it is; all the instruments are perfect just as they are. There is no point in trying to make a trumpet sound like a flute or to make a violin sound like the piano, and unfortunately that was what I had been doing. Developing staff had been focused on making them proficient in every single area of the business (a sneaky way to find yourself focusing on the areas your staff members are least proficient in). From this vision, I realized that the way to experience the music and harmony was about seeing the natural talent and focusing the majority of my energy there. This new focus would then bring the instruments into harmony, working at the same tempo; aware of each other and what they uniquely contributed to the whole.

I realized that by trying to make a flute a trumpet, I was doing a major disservice to my employees and my team. Up until that point, the direction I had was to train them in every area and make them experts. This was of course a method for my company to hedge their bets and make sure a store could function under any circumstance that occurred. Eventually, I threw all that knowledge out the door and started to create my own through seeking the gift/strength in each employee. From this new focus my mood changed, my training changed, and so did every other developmental model I used in business. It felt like magic when we all were fully tuned, in tempo, and a truly harmonious orchestra. But once again this isn't magic, it's truly understanding the mind and learning new skills and techniques to support us on our paths.

The crazy thing? It had been a spiritual self-development journey up until that point, and much of my efforts to become "enlightened" had a very counterproductive effect on my actual state of *being*. I had continually focused all my efforts on "becoming more" without ever celebrating what I already was. I was an instrument as well, and through that process I had also changed to focusing on the strength within me.

I know how important this is, and I also know how EASY it is to LOSE sight of focusing on the strength (both in yourself and in others). This isn't about living in an imaginary world where you avoid and ignore negative behaviors. Rather, it's about living in a space where you seek to see the best and focus on that best behavior being demonstrated. This doesn't require visualization or imagination at all; it requires heartfelt focus to actually see a person in their totality.

Our minds are beyond powerful. In many ways, when it comes to the ability to guide our minds it's like we are learning to drive for the first time. The unfortunate thing is that we aren't learning this in a parking lot of the mall with a parent right there to guide us or step in. Instead, we are learning this all in a really fast sports car in the middle of a racetrack, typically by ourselves. Getting our focus and keeping it tuned without getting lost among our many thoughts and chatter is hard work. We simply need to be kind to ourselves and create the beautiful reminders that can point us along our journey over and over again. You are your guide, and you need to guide yourself over and over and over again.

The Vision Sheet supports you to see your year in a way that opens you up to the possibilities and growth. Adding to this, you start to consciously create and guide yourself by learning to identify the true feeling you want to experience in your life. It is ultimately the feeling and the experience that we are always after, but most of the time we take actions that don't lead us to the end result we seek. This is why we will be practicing how to identify the energy you seek, align it with the cosmos, and discover the actions you can take that will get you there.

Vision Sheet Instructions
Emotional Direction

Working with the information you have gathered, you are now prepared to consciously set a vision/intention for your year.

Step I:

Each of the 12 houses in astrology represents an area of life where energy gets expressed. You will be using the 12 houses to guide you in creating a FEELING you would like to experience for the upcoming year.

Part 1:

Turn to the backside of the Vision Sheet and locate the circle at the top of the page. There are 12 segments in the circle that correspond to the 12 astrological houses. You will be writing in the feeling that you would like to experience in that area of your life for this year.

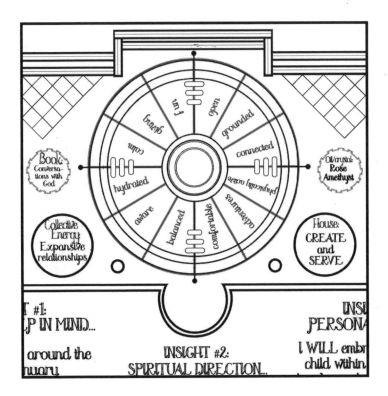

Part 2:

Below is a simple reference point for each house. Your job now is to pick the feeling/emotion that you want to call in for your upcoming year. You will be picking one word or short phrase to capture the experience you want to have. First, you will read the reference point by house below and then pick a feeling/experience that comes to you in that area of your life. Keep it simple, positive, uplifting, and achievable!

HOUSE 1: Physical Body

HOUSE 2: Finances/Resources

HOUSE 3: Hobbies

HOUSE 4: Home Environment

HOUSE 5: Play

HOUSE 6: Daily Habits

HOUSE 7: Relationships

HOUSE 8: Spiritual Development

HOUSE 9: Educational

HOUSE 10: Career

HOUSE 11: Charitable Work

HOUSE 12: Artistic Expression

STEP 2:

Now that you have identified the feelings you are wanting to call into your experience, flip to the front of the page to determine the three most active houses (the ones with the most planets in them) from your calendar.

Part 1:

Take a moment to connect the dots on the feelings you want to call in AND the houses that are most active for your year. Once you've determined the three most active houses, go ahead and highlight or outline them on the back. This will show you the three core feelings you are wanting to experience for your year that are being activated by the cosmos as well.

STEP 3:

I wouldn't be a very good Taurus if I left you in the fuzzy space with nothing to apply to your life! With these three feelings and three houses AND all the information you've gathered in this book, it's time to set some goals. Here is the thing about goals: They are meant to be achievable! This is about stretching and building up your spiritual strength (not living in *la la land* and hoping for the best).

Part 1:

Look at the feeling that you have intended for your year and the area of life that this is connected to. Ask yourself: What action could I take to support me to feel this way?

Part 2:

When you start to generate ideas around the actions that you can take, you will pick just one action for your three goals. A good action will be:

- Something that is measurable, meaning you can easily determine if you took the action or not.
- Something that is achievable, meaning you know that you could achieve the goal if you put the effort forth.
- Something with an appropriate time frame or duration for the goal to be achieved.

For instance, let's look at a common goal that people often have: being less judgmental. This is not actually a goal because it does not meet the criteria above. The not being judgmental is completely subjective, and there is no actionable task that you would be able to hold yourself accountable to. Instead, if the desire is to be less judgmental, you build a goal that supports that state. For instance, you could commit to journal writing for five minutes each day on acceptance and how you consciously practiced that in your specific daily interactions. If you selected the time frame of two weeks for this goal, you would know you achieved your goal if you had 14 journal entries at the end of that time.

Part 3:

Once you have your three goals, you can write them on the Vision Sheet or put them somewhere special. Now the only thing you need to do is commit and see them through. Don't worry if it feels heavy to start in a new direction; that heaviness won't last long. The more you move in the direction, the quicker the energy will begin to move. This will eventually activate what's called the Law of Momentum: Energy in motion tends to stay in motion. You are a creator after all! It's hard work at times, but well worth it!

CREATING A LARGER VISION BOARD

If you would like to continue the energy you have built around this Vision Sheet, you can use it as an anchor for a larger yearly Vision Board. Please do not worry; you do not need to be incredibly creative or crafty to turn this Vision Sheet quickly into a Vision Board! The true power of the Vision Board isn't in the length of time it takes you to make it, but in the consciousness intention you have when you create it.

A Vision Board works because it supports clearing the energy and focusing your consciousness in a specific direction. It allows you to take one step forward, and as we all know, the one step forward creates new energy and new circumstances. It creates a visual representation of the energetics you are seeking to experience (not just of things, but of emotions and experiences). Seeing your year and envisioning it isn't about manifesting the things your Ego desires. It is about connecting in at a Soul level to embrace your journey and move forward on the most expansive path. These are the only guidelines I would like to share with you on this process: create a Vision Board through your Higher Self (Soul/Spirit), and make it fill you up with the feeling of inspiration.

There is no right or wrong way to make a Vision Board. Release any judgment you have around this, because anyone can do this in any way they please. I have included my ideas below to support you, but there are many ways and none of them are right or wrong.

VISION BOARD IDEAS:

- [My favorite] This option allows you to create the Vision Board quickly (in 10 minutes or less) and leaves you with the ability to add to it throughout your entire year! You can create your Vision Board digitally and can create this through Pinterest or in a program on your computer. First, you will take pictures with your phone of the Vision Sheet. Take some close-up photos, as well as some from faraway. Be inspired. You can upload these photos to your computer or straight onto a private/public Pinterest board. Once you get your images from your Vision Sheet uploaded, you can work to find other pins that you like and keep adding to your Vision Board all year long. Check out the cool things to include below.

- You can alternatively create a collage on poster board or use a bulletin board, using the Vision Sheet and other inspiring images of your choosing. I think this process works best if you print out and have all the images ready before you actually sit down to begin to make your collage. You can read the ideas of what to include in what follows and create a piece of art that represents the energy of your year and what you are seeking to experience. Remember to infuse it with emotions, and focus on experiences to guide you. Some supplies you will need: poster board, pens, markers, pictures, glue, magazines, etc.

NOTE: This method is very powerful when you are working with a group of people and want to create your Vision Boards together. This happens with friends who have birthdays close together OR if you work with a team of people who have a project coming up and simply want to make a Vision Board to inspire everyone. If you do decide to do a Vision Board in a group, have each person bring a few items to the gathering for everyone to use when they create their boards (or one large group board).

COOL THINGS YOU CAN INCLUDE:

- Find motivational quotes and personal pictures that speak to you, and add them into your Vision Board.
- If there is something you are wanting to create and bring into your life, find a representation of that and add it into your Vision Board (if it makes you feel good).
- Chose a color and theme for your Vision Board to inspire your year (whenever you wear that color you will be connecting back in with your intentions).
- Don't limit yourself, and make sure to think outside the box. Give a smell and feeling to your year. You may think a smell is farfetched, but how fun! If you truly channel the smell and bring it in, you will be surprised at the emotions a scent can carry for you. You can easily spray a physical board with your new favorite perfume, and for a digital Vision Board, add the picture of the scent in whatever way you can. You can literally wear the scent as you make the board! What will happen is that you are literally energetically charging the board and creating an energy shortcut. What you will find is that when you wear the perfume again, you are wearing much more than the scent!
- Create an energetic timeline of the last year to allow yourself to see the continued growth of your path. Do this with lots of detail or very little—it doesn't matter. Celebrate the year you just moved through, and take time to recognize that movement. We spend far too-much time thinking about the distance between where we are and where we want to go than we ever do looking at where we've come from. Know you are moving forward on your path, and don't be too shy to celebrate all the movement you've already accomplished.

The idea with a Vision Board is that you are making space in the physical world to recognize the vision you see for your year. In my experience, creating a Vision Board makes a significant difference in how you will experience your year and how you will reach its true potential. With all the cosmic guidance and your Vision Sheet, you will be tapping into something much larger than yourself and calling it into your being.

I solidified this very simple approach to working with the yearly energies because I believe it is the most powerful way to do so. There is a magical place of balance with astrology: give too much and you've lost it; give too little and there is nothing to grasp onto. The true wisdom is in the balance, and I have found this to be true of all things.

When your birthdate comes around yet again, you can choose to reread the entire book or you can simply proceed to the condensed Vision Sheet instructions that are at the end of the book. Always choose the process that feels the most inspiring and fills you with excitement. If this book has made a difference for you and elevates your year, please consider paying it forward. I can imagine no better gift for the spiritual seeker on their birthday than the ability to align with the cosmos and ignite their path.

X

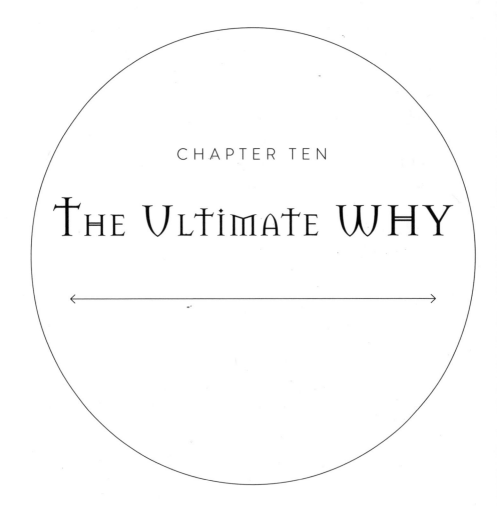

CHAPTER TEN

The Ultimate WHY

If you're anything like me, you'll see that this all works and you'll need to know why. You will want to have that understanding and knowing in your heart because you crave it. It's as if you will lock in right now to these words and be ready to receive the energy, the insight, and the new perspective. You are ready and you are willing to learn, understand, and grow.

Astrology works because we are (all of us) a part of the same organism or consciousness. Consciousness exists within larger fields of consciousness, and all of it is birthed from the all that is. The creation from the all that is, which includes us and the entire Universe, was created using patterns. Many people are aware of sacred geometry, fractals, and the symmetry that is in the creation of all things. The patterns that were present at the moment of your birth and from your exact vantage point on Earth reflect the pattern that is ultimately you. The movement that then takes place to the pattern that is YOU after you arrive is created by You and still develops along the lines of the larger patterns. It is much like a kaleidoscope or tapestry of energetic choices, and while all of them exist, you are focusing in on a path right now and choosing which one to move into rhythm with.

Astrology is a method of interpretation (much like words that symbolize things) that focuses on understanding these patterns and the implication they have on our experiences (it allows you to see choices and opportunities that are available for you to embrace). We are each creating our reality and our experience, but we often forget that we are active participants in the unfolding. Allowing the patterns to reveal deeper truths to you will support you on your journey because they can open doors simply by letting you know that the doors exist. For me personally, I never would have aligned with my passion of writing if not for astrology. It was through my birth chart that I gained the courage to take that first step, and I am forever grateful for the insight and wisdom of this ancient practice.

The gift and the curse that we all experience in our lives is that we start from a space of amnesia, fully separated from the all that is. It is a gift because it allows us the experience of ourselves. It is a curse because when you are separate from the all that is and you have forgotten all of this, you begin to identify yourself with the things around you. Most often, you fully identify yourself as the Inner Speaker in your head. Painfully, you begin to believe what that Inner Speaker says, and forget to question, challenge, adapt, and change your thoughts. Those thoughts you think have creative power, and when they have a mind of their own it can be very uncomfortable to be present in your own life.

I remember reading spiritual books and wanting them to just give me the answer. Why couldn't I just figure the whole thing out? And of course no one can give you the answer, because this is not a thing that you figure out. You might be wondering: What is the all that is and how am I not the I that I thought I was? I can say to you that those are very good questions and that you are on your path and calling the answers to you. You most certainly are a spiritual being, and you are here at the Soul Level/Perspective having a human experience. The experience is the point and an awakening to your Spirit to be one with the experience in the present moment of now is the ultimate point.

True awakening isn't about gaining control over everybody and everything. It isn't about manifesting fame or fortune and learning how to use universal laws for egoic gain. Awakening is witnessing the creative force in all things (GOD).

God does not play God—God merely sees God.

The beauty has never been in the having of things or the acquiring of things. I remembered this Soul wisdom when I took my pilgrimage across Spain. A beautiful journey from Saint-Jean-Pied-de-Porte to Santiago, where I lost two toenails, fought food poisoning, and abandoned 50 percent of the things I brought from my backpack on the second day.

The saddest/happiest part of that experience was when I arrived and completed the pilgrimage. That's when I remembered. I loved and grew through the journey: the smell of the air, the cold water on my swollen feet, and the moments of complete freedom and inner silence.

None of what we truly love is quantifiable or physical. The experience is the gift, never the thing.

The trouble is, the ability to understand all of this doesn't come through the thinking mind. I always use my words to describe the indescribable things I'm experiencing, because I remember when I was aching to have someone share this with me. All I do with my writing is in hopes that these words will support those who are seekers, and perhaps point a way that serves you. I cannot hand you peace or knowing. It's not mine to give, and I don't have it—I experience it in beautiful moments within.

There will be various phases and truths that you move through on your path. Hold on loosely through the awakening process, and always fall back into your heart. A constantly thinking mind is a part of awakening, but it is not what guides you through (it's the noise that wakes you up). You will make mistakes, but they aren't mistakes. You will feel like you are moving in circles, but they are actually spirals. Those spirals? They are infinity loops of the all that is.

You will think you have lost your way, only to realize you were never lost.

At the end of the day, you KNOW you are Spirit in a human body. You are absolutely being guided by YOU, and everything is unfolding as it should. The path is a wild one full of love, humor, upset, and pain. It is a path of never-ending opportunity, endless growth, and beautiful moments captured in time.

Never forget: The gift of life is *life*.

QUICK GUIDE

←——————————————————————→

Vision Sheet Instructions

Please use these instructions when you want to move quickly and efficiently in setting up the front side of your yearly vision sheet.

PHASE I: Basic Set Up Instructions

Step 1: Write the time frame you are exploring into the blank innermost circle on the front page of your Vision Sheet. For instance, if you are exploring the year 2017, you will write in the time frame, 2017–2018.

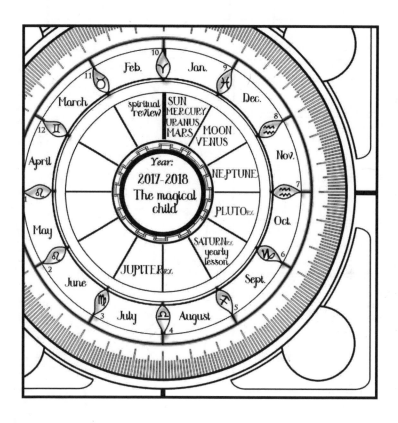

Step 2: On the front page of your Vision Sheet, there is a circle chart in the center with rectangles on either side where you will write in the dates for your year. Starting with the rectangle on the left labeled " I," write your birthdate into the blank rectangle and add the 30-day time period. For example, if you were born on February 21, your first time span in the 1st rectangle would be "February 21–March 21."

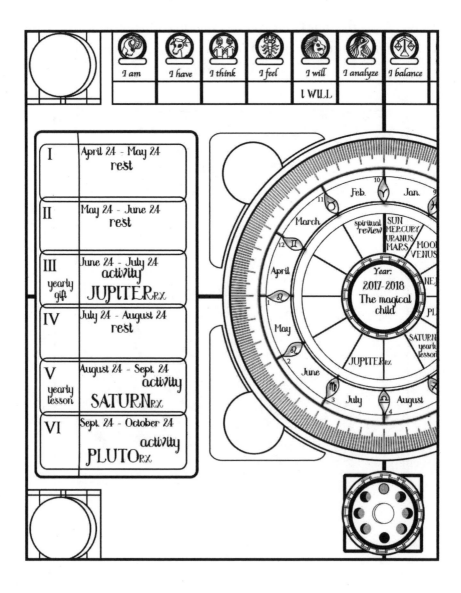

Step 3: You will continue this pattern until you have created your 12-month breakdown for your cosmic calendar. Reference the example copy on pages 14–15 if needed.

PHASE 2: Enter the Planets, See the Pattern

Step 1: In table 1, column 1, of your Cosmic Navigator, you will find the names of the relevant planets, and under column 4 you will see the astrological house location. Once you locate the number in the "Annual House" column, write the planet name into the larger connected rectangle on your Vision Sheet.

* Do this for all of the planets: Sun, Moon, Mercury, Venus, Mars, Jupiter, Saturn, Uranus, Neptune & Pluto.

Step 2: By now you have a very nice visual of how the energy is spread out for your year through the energetic patterning. Rectangles with no planets represent time frames when the energy tends to be more constrictive, and is typically a time when you will want to consciously choose to take it easy, slow down, and relax. Locate the rectangles that have no planets, and write in the word "relax" to remind yourself to honor the slower moments of the year by regrouping, relaxing, and taking care of yourself.

Step 3: Rectangles with planets represent time frames of activity in your life. Locate the rectangles that have planets or sensitive points and write in the word "activity" to remind yourself that you can align with the energy of the planet by remaining aware and ready to experience the energy as it shows up.

* You can read more about the constrictive and expansive energy on page 19.

PHASE 3: Yearly Lesson & Yearly Gift

Step 1: Locate Saturn in the rectangles, and write in the words "Yearly Lesson" under the roman numeral. There is always a nugget of wisdom to be absorbed during this time frame if you are able to expand your perspective and grasp it.

Step 2: Locate Jupiter in the rectangles and write in the words "Yearly Gift" under the roman numeral. There is always a great form of expansion that takes place through the energy of Jupiter (whether you recognize it or not).

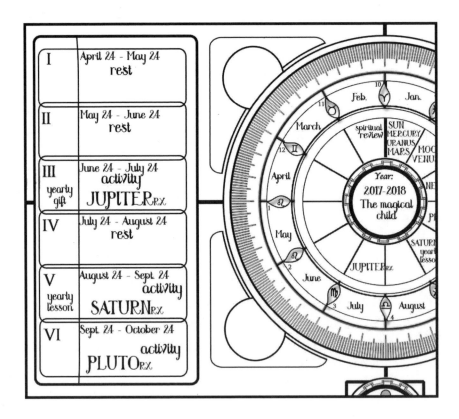

Step 3: Visually take in the energetic patterning and begin to discover the impact of each planet. You may reference the Planet Key on page 33 to further explore the energetic dynamics present in your year.

PHASE 4: Spiritual Review (Growth point)

Step 1: Look to table 1, columns 1 and 4, of your Cosmic Navigator to determine the Annual house location of the Sun (where your spiritual review will take place). You can enter "Spiritual Review" into the appropriate house location of your Vision Sheet. See the example Vision Sheet for reference if needed.

* To learn more about HOW this energy will express throughout your year go to page 42.

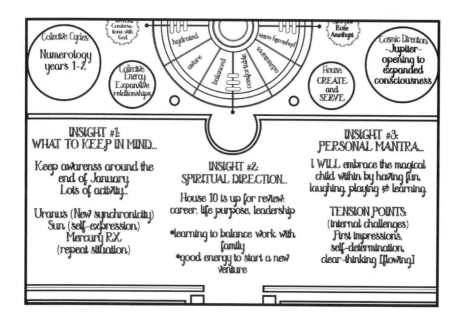

PHASE 5: YOUR YEARLY APPROACH

Step 1: Look to table 1, columns 1 and 2, of your Cosmic Navigator to determine the Ascendant (a.k.a. Rising Sign) in your yearly chart. Read more about its impact on page 63 and pick one archetype it is associated with and enter it into the middle circle of your Vision Sheet.

Step 2: At the top of the Vision Sheet there is a list of the 12 signs and the personal power phrase associated with each sign. You can highlight the ascendant/rising sign of your chart by entering in the personal power phrase into the appropriate box. For example, if your rising sign is Aries, you would write in, "I AM."

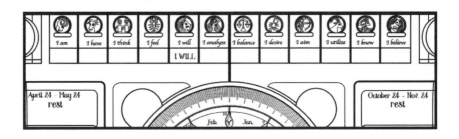

PHASE 6: STAY AWARE

Astrology is meant to support you on your path and provide insights when you need them. Keep this Vision Sheet accessible and be ready to tap into the power of the cosmos whenever you need it!

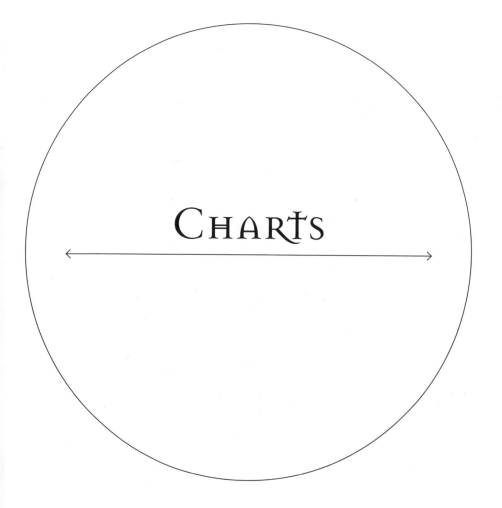

CHARTS

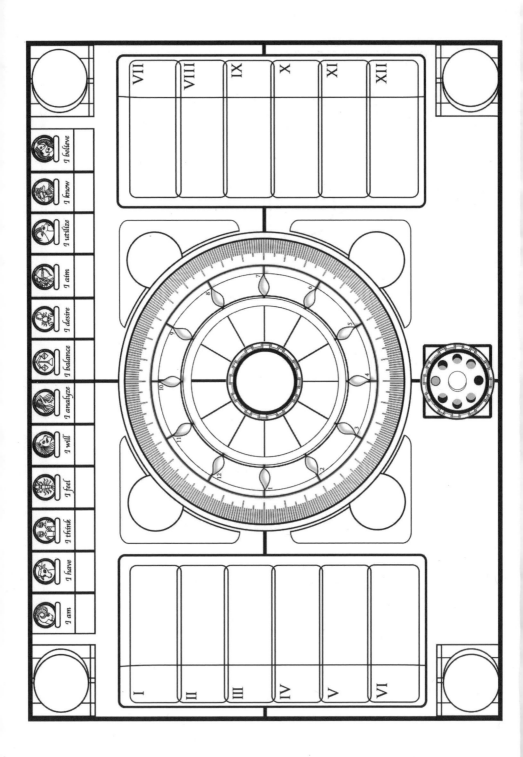

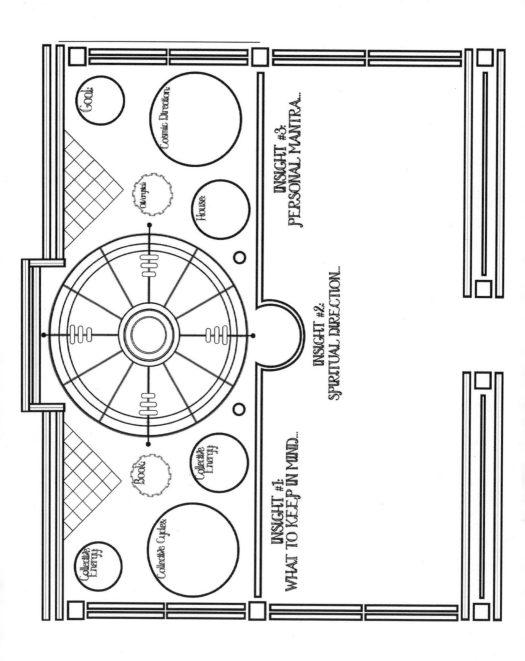

Goal:

Cosmic Direction:

Olympus:

House:

INSIGHT #3:
PERSONAL MANTRA...

INSIGHT #2:
SPIRITUAL DIRECTION...

INSIGHT #1:
WHAT TO KEEP IN MIND...

Books:

Collective
Energy

Collective
Energy

Collective Cycles

Visit www.absolutelyastrology.com now to download your Cosmic Navigator, Vision Sheet and Sample Vision Sheet!